Mysterious Sedona

Tom Dongo

With thanks!
Tom Dongo

Published by
Hummingbird Press

Cover design by
Tom Dongo

ISBN 0-9622748-6-0

Published by
Hummingbird Press
P.O. Box 2571
Sedona, AZ 86339

Printed by
Sedona Color Graphics

Dedication

For Canyon Kevin. May him and his kind,
children of the Earth, live forever in the winds.
And never be forgotten.

Contents

Preface

My introduction to Tom Dongo came within one year of the first time I visited Sedona during the summer of 1989, between the completion of my own book [*Mass Dreams of the Future* (Author's note: an international bestseller)] and its initial hard-cover publication by Mc Graw Hill & Co. that November. At the time, ignoring my earlier future visions of living in northern Arizona during times of cataclysmic change, I'd bought a rustic cabin in southern California's San Bernardino mountains instead. I spent nearly a week in Sedona in late July 1989, fascinated by its Red Rock beauty, Native American connections and unusual energy vortex points, which back then were often marked by beautiful, hand-crafted "medicine wheels:" stone circles created and cared for by residents and tourists alike. One could therefore easily locate these special vibration spots, then far more than the six or seven "official" sites listed in books or marked on hand-out maps today. This was before the US Forest Service decided that somehow by marking these areas people desecrated the "natural landscape" and began systematically destroying them, often messing up the ground it claimed to be preserving far more than the stone circles ever did.

In fact, I personally think that this campaign, begun in the mid-1990's and culminating in a lengthy "battle" over the Grand-daddy of these modern medicine wheels just off Schnebly Hill Road, marked a critical (although largely unheralded) transition for the Red Rock Country as people were deliberately pushed away from natural, spontaneous and spiritual contact with this ancient sacred land into today's "managed" tourism of time shares, jeep tours, ear-shattering helicopter rides, paved trail heads with on-trail-only hiking and New Age eco-walks. Now, we're about to have parking fees imposed on us at all forest entry points as the Federal bureaucracy and local Chamber of Commerce team up to separate us further and further from the land, while still loudly proclaiming that it belongs to "we, the people".

So, it's both with nostalgia and pride that I note that my long-time Sedona resident and friend Tom Dongo continues to proclaim the strange, unusual, off-the-wall, and sometimes downright scary goings-on that punctuate life for many here among the Red Rocks and Verde Valley. The latest in a series of well-written and best-selling volumes that started over a decade ago with *The Mysteries of Sedona* [1988] and *The Alien Tide* [my autographed copy is dated July 28, 1990, when I first met Tom at a talk at the Center for the New Age], the book you have in your hands not only updates Tom & Linda's outstanding research of the paranormal phenomena observed at the Bradshaw Ranch in recent years [see their book, *Merging Dimensions*] but also chronicles many of the strange experiences residents and tourists alike have had while spontaneously exploring the back canyons and vortex sites in and around Sedona. These stories are light years away from our "managed tourism's" cute Western snap-shots and remind us that there remains far more magic and mystery to this beautiful area than the bureaucrats or established commercial interests want to acknowledge or permit.

My wife Kallista and myself, Sedona home-owners since April 1994, have had our share of similar experiences here over the last six years, often kept private because who wants to create a circus-like atmosphere around one's home? And we are not alone; many of our local friends plus visitors who've attended one of the *Crystal Healing* or *Earth Mysteries* conferences we've hosted here in recent years have told us fascinating tales of unexplained encounters, both psychic and physical, almost always when they slipped away from crowded tourist centers and struck out on their own—doing just what the "powers-that-be" want to discourage.

We've also noted a significant change in UFO and "Black Ops." activity that has occurred since we moved here. At that time our house, a former healing center nestled beneath Airport Mesa in West Sedona and once home to the Hopi elder, White Bear [*Book of the Hopi*], regularly witnessed fly-overs by large numbers of almost-silent black or olive camouflaged helicopters, heading north towards the Secret Canyon Wilderness area. This activity abruptly stopped shortly after the late-July 1994 "Lost Fire" there. Personal friends, one of whom was then in training with the Sedona fire department, told us of receiving very-strange orders NOT to get involved in fighting that blaze— unheard of in a naturally arid, windy region like ours where uncontrolled forest fires are disastrous. Is it a coincidence that another friend told of seeing Vice President Al Gore at the local restaurant where she was a waitress that week? His visit was *not* mentioned in the press. Since that summer the almost-silent camouflaged helicopters have been replaced by very noisy tourist-bearing machines that regularly wake us up on Sunday mornings. And, six years later, most of the reported UFO activity seems to have shifted from the northern Secret Canyon area to the west towards Dry Creek and south near Bell Rock, although we've still noticed huge "Mother ships" occasionally appearing over Sedona itself—usually as fast-moving "stars" that defy conventional aircraft, satellite or meteorite behavior, hovering or changing course or suddenly blinking out when observed in our still-clear night sky.

In June 1998, when my wife left for her parents' home in France a week before my own annual departure to research English Crop Circles, thereby leaving me a temporary bachelor, I had the privilege of joining Tom Dongo and Linda Bradshaw for an evening's sky-watch out at the Bradshaw Ranch. As usual, it was a crisp, clear night and the stars were gorgeous. Following Tom's instructions, I brought a cheap flash camera with me with a 36 roll of 100 ASA color film. The three of us spent a couple of hours walking around the grounds with the dogs, talking about my research on Crop Circles and Regression therapy, which I practice here in Sedona when time permits. Every now and then, prompted by some internal and invisible instinct, Linda would point her camera at the horizon and squeeze off a flash shot. Often the dogs would react at the same moment, racing off in the direction she turned to. Following her lead, I began to snap off shots in the same general direction, or sometimes when Tom would suddenly do the same thing. Once or twice it seemed as if we heard branches snapping in the distance after we'd all turned and shot off our flash cameras, although we never actually saw anything suspicious moving about. On two occasions we did see the mysterious "Sedona lights" referred to in this book hovering and pulsating at the horizon but as soon as we raised our cameras, they disappeared. It didn't seem like a lot of activity but soon I'd finished the roll of film and it was time to return home. Imagine my amazement and delight when the developed photos came back 24 hours later. Although 33 of the 36 shots were black (a small flash like that is useless for night distance shots), the three others each contained white globes—one was especially distinct with the other two were sort of hazy or off-center. And we'd never seen a thing physically! The sensation I felt on opening up that package of photos remains a high point of my time in Sedona, even today.

In a way, opening up this book is similar to what I went through that day. At first you may not notice anything too far from the ordinary, especially if you live here, but as you read on into the "meat" of this literary feast, you will catch a glimpse of what the tourist managers want you to ignore: tales of high strangeness and awesome experiences as time, space and energy dimensions connect here in magical, mystical Sedona. Thanks, Tom, for reminding us again that, in Sedona at least, "Nothing is exactly what it appears to be."

Dr. Chet Snow
P.O. Box 1738
Sedona AZ 86339

Foreword

I've been writing books and magazine articles for almost thirty years—off and on. During this time I have always wanted to write something that was not in the final stretch altered by the adventurous red pen of an editor. Somewhere on this planet is an editor, man or woman, who can edit something without re-writing it. I've never met one. If such a person exists I should write a book about him or her. An editor might change—or omit—one perfectly good keyword in a chapter and it can alter the meaning and direction of the whole chapter, and sometimes the entire book. Editors can take a spirited manuscript and when they are through with it, the work can read like a computer manual.

Any writer who deals with editors on a regular basis will tell you exactly the same thing. But don't get me totally wrong. Editors absolutely have a place. A seasoned editor can take a rather bad manuscript with possibilities and turn it into a very good manuscript.

I'm saying all of this somewhat tongue-in-cheek—of course—because a few editors along the long road have literally saved my literary Butt in a number of near fatally embarrassing situations. Some of my best friends are editors—I even went to dinner with one once.

However and nevertheless, what you will read in this book is exactly what I meant and how I meant it. Unedited. So it may be the last book I ever write—or the first. Grammar freaks be forewarned, this is written in the free style of novelists. I have always envied the unfettered style of the novelist. They can get away with just about anything. I think few novelists worry much about editors. If you are not sure what I'm talking about, read some of William Faulkner's novels—and he won a Nobel Prize for literature in 1949. . . . .

Photo taken in 1998 near Sedona by Cheryl Dryfka.

CHAPTER ONE

Mysterious Sedona

Whenever I write a book about the paranormal I have to be very creative with rearranging manuscripts to keep it from reading like a patchwork quilt. I will have a section of a book or a whole book almost finished when some new story or information drops in my lap that must be included in the book. Keeping a smooth, continuous flow in a manuscript can be a real challenge. That happened again today.

I have the habit of going to a coffee shop around 10:00 a.m. and drinking a couple of quality cups of coffee and reading a newspaper cover to cover. I'm kind of well known for that around here. And Sedona does have excellent coffee shops with excellent coffee now. As I've said over the years I am not easy to find and one of the ways people have tracked me down in the past is to ask around at the coffee shops. I used to do this coffee ritual every day religiously but now I do 10:00 a.m. coffee only about twice a week.

I stopped by a west Sedona bakery this morning for coffee and was told that a man from Iceland had been looking for me since 7:30 a.m.. I thought it must be important if someone is going to that much trouble to find me. This sort of thing has happened many times over the past ten years. It was a nice sunny day so I was sitting outside under an umbrella table drinking my coffee and met the fellow. His name was Gadar. He was a very young looking guy of thirty-eight with his tall, slim and pretty blond wife with startling ice blue eyes whose name was Signa. Signa seemed to be about ten years younger than Gadar. She didn't speak English very well but he was fluent.

I'm always waiting to hear some story that would blow my socks off. It's happened a couple of times. So when

Gadar said he had an experience in Secret Canyon my interest really perked up.

Before I tell you what he told me, I need to mention that I have heard the same manner of story he was about to tell me a thousand times in the past in different versions. But he and his wife were obviously exceptionally bright and successful people and they had taken valuable time from their holiday to locate me. So to him—and me—it was an exceedingly important story.

It seems that, in 1991, on an earlier trip to Sedona, Gadar had been traveling with a group of people from New Jersey and Iceland. One day eight of the group had hiked into Secret Canyon. They had gone quite a ways into Secret Canyon and finding a comfortable spot, they lay down for awhile to rest. Gadar remarked that not long after he felt some sort of presence and opened his eyes. He said that hovering above the slumbering group was a flying saucer— a UFO. As he watched, he said a beam came from the craft. The beam hit Gadar on the top of his head and penetrated down through all of his chakras and stopped at his base chakra. He was told by a voice in his head that "they" were doing work on his chakra system as a gift to him. So at this point I asked the inevitable question I always ask: "Was the ship physical and did the rest of the group also see the ship?"

Gadar replied that, no, the ship was not physical. He seemed to be the only one to see it. But, he pointed out, the others in the group felt an unmistakable presence close by and told him so.

Gadar returned to the same general area the next night by himself and had another, near identical experience as the day before with the UFO. He also had some strange alien like visions in the following several days.

So here is my point in bringing this up. Like I said, I have heard this story told by hundreds of people in a thousand different ways. So what's up? The majority of these people having these experiences are college educated, highly intelligent, successful and most of them are well-grounded, common sense people.

Most told their story with difficulty as if they really didn't want to talk about it but had to. I am also well known, far and wide, as a good listener. I never ridicule anyone or make light of their story, no matter what the content may be.

These people cannot all be hallucinating and/or making up these kinds of stories. There are just too many people, probably in the millions, ultimately. So we are left with the evidence that something awesome is going on. But what the direction and ultimate meaning of it all is, I for one, do not have a simple or clear answer.

But it's real. In this book I will raise many pointed questions but will have few black and white answers. Over the years I have encountered numerous people who claimed to have all the answers. But in reality, I discovered most had none. Believe nothing until you yourself can prove it to be true.

Are we, as a collective, supposed by design to discover on our own the answers to the ultimate questions? If so, then what? What lies ahead after we make the realization?

There is an element in the subconscious of many people which utterly refuses to accept the existence of non-human beings or events or objects beyond their reality, even when confronted with evidence that would convince a normal open minded person.

I've said this before in many things I have written: if skeptics, or even believers, could experience even a few of the most dramatic sightings, events, or encounters that I have then this world would be full of people trying in every way possible to get to the bottom of this awesome, life changing enigma.

But it might be that many of us who are interested may be basically looking in the wrong direction. It may be that current evidence has caused us to look at the smoke and not the fire. And, is the fire some sort of existence that we barely have the consciousness and perhaps the intelligence to understand? I wonder. How hard have we looked?

What you will read in this book is the truth. Some of it is so bizarre it can't possibly be true—according to normal belief structures. But it is all true. I will present these stories just as I and others have experienced them. The subjects I write about are often defiantly serious so perhaps in this book as opposed to some of my others I can give these stories greater personality, meaning and depth.

This book is an extension of my last book, *Merging Dimensions*, which I co-wrote with Linda Bradshaw. Linda is now divorced and in 1997 moved to northern Montana. The divorce is not the result of paranormal activity that had occurred on the Bradshaw Ranch. (In 1999 she remarried in Montana).

Many of the most important events and photos which were related to *Merging Dimensions* (released in the Spring of 1995) occurred in the weeks and months directly after *Merging Dimensions* had appeared in print. Nearly all of that evidence is included in this book, though this book is in every sense a part of the Mysterious Sedona enigma.

I was planning to do a separate book, eventually, which I was going to call the *Incredible Sedona Lights*. I have instead included nearly all of that evidence and information in this book.

I have one of the world's largest collections of paranormal photographs. Perhaps even the largest. Most of these photographs have been examined by the best photo experts alive. For the most part the experts are simply baffled. Any photo that is and was an obvious hoax or the possible result of some sort of defect got tossed out early on. Most of the photos were taken in this area but many are from other areas around the world. The hundreds that I have are truly ultra extraordinary photographs.

When *Merging Dimensions* was published we never realized how much the impact of the book was going to be lessened because the photos in the main body of the book had to be in black and white. This was for financial reasons because all color photos are incredibly expensive to reproduce. Had we printed the book in color, the book would have had to sell in the $30.00 range instead of $14.95.

Many of those who had read *Merging Dimensions* were astounded at the stunning impact of the photos when they later saw the full color photos in my collection. Every one of them offered that the book lost so much because of the black and white photos in it. Linda and I have an excellent agent in New York City. He tried to sell a book project of photos and stories which included *Merging Dimensions,* to a major publishing house with the idea of making it into a new all-color book.

Almost all of the publishers contacted were seriously interested. The book project made it to a number of final decision meetings of some of the largest publishing houses in New York. But in the end they were afraid to buy it because of the avant garde strangeness of the photos and stories. No doubt from the fear that there would be some sort of negative backlash against it. Skeptic attacks, religious groups, etc. Even though we had agreed to have JPL Laboratories check out the photos for authenticity—in the event the photos and manuscript were sold.

Ten or twenty years ago major publishers would stick their necks out a mile for an unusual, promising manuscript. But these days unless they think it will be a hugely profitable best-seller, they won't risk anything. The project is now pretty much a dead issue. However, when Linda Bradshaw and I were gathering photos and written material for *Merging Dimensions,* we thought it would surely be a good investment for we felt that *Merging Dimensions* would be a best seller on the photos alone. So did a lot of other well-placed people. Our agent, who is one of the longest surviving literary agents and publishers in New York, felt the same way after he saw the project that was presented. *Merging Dimensions* was the pivotal part of the project. He said there has never, ever, before been a book like *Merging Dimensions. Merging Dimensions,* for all the worldwide excitement it created at the time has sold poorly. Perhaps it was a case of "before it's time." I don't know.

Linda and I put every available dollar we had into the research project which would ultimately become the book *Merging Dimensions.* Because of the evidence we were coming up with we thought that surely some wealthy paranormal buff would become interested and supply the funds and equipment we so desperately needed. It didn't happen. We, or interested friends, contacted some of the wealthiest individuals and foundations on this planet. Several individuals, known to have a great interest in the paranormal, were multi-billionaires. After a huge effort we got nowhere. It almost seemed like something "out there" was making sure our efforts wouldn't work. We have some rather disturbing and confirming evidence of that. There is an unspeakable pity involved here. There was an eight month or so period in 1996, when on any night one could go to the area we were conducting our research in and witness events and sights that few people on this planet will ever have the opportunity to experience. In this book I will describe most of those events. During that time we had only the barest of equipment. That eight month window passed and what could have been learned for the whole planet during that time?

I think contact with an unknown deep space or interdimensional race or races, or an alien life form, was entirely possible. It may be an absolute truth that they were trying to contact us during that time but a means—or way—was not established. Although, that opportunity may not have been lost, it certainly has been dramatically diminished.

I've emphasized this eight month period in the hope that should a similar paranormal scenario appear again somewhere in the world, it won't again be overlooked by scientists. What I will present in this book is a contribution, but it will never have the credibility impact that nuts and bolts scientific research and hard to question scientific evidence could have had. Especially if "credentialed" persons were directly involved in the research project.

While at the height of much of this activity, we invited all sorts of well known psychics, contactees, abductees, UFO researchers, channelers, writers, and others out to the Bradshaw Ranch just to see what might happen. Not much did while those people were there, but one thing we discovered was that if there were more than four or five people in the area, usually absolutely nothing happened. Whoever "they" were they didn't like crowds. However, animals didn't bother "them" in the least. There were plenty of dogs, horses, and cattle with us and around us and it made no difference.

One unusual incident, however, involved Joy Gilbert who

has written a book on being abducted by aliens (benevolent) and is a popular speaker who lectures widely. While we were at the ranch with Joy Gilbert not much of a dramatic nature happened. We tried the usual stuff like calling things in, meditating, flashing lights to the sky, remote viewing, visualizing, and other methods. We saw a few odd distant lights flying around but that was all.

So about midnight (this was in the summer of 1996) we called it a day. Joy had ridden in with me in my full-sized Dodge van. We were about halfway back to Sedona on the Boynton Pass Road which is gravel, narrow and rough. We were talking about something having to do with aliens when a bright flash to my left caught my attention. I had to stick my head out the driver's side window and look back towards the rear of my van to see what the flash was. Joy couldn't see in that direction because there were no windows on the left side of the van. What I saw, about fifty yards out from the back of the van, was a huge, softly glowing silvery object. The huge object was just above the tree tops and was exactly matching the speed of my van. I didn't watch the strange object long because I drove off the road into the desert and had to twist the wheel hard to get back onto the road. Luckily I didn't hit anything or damage the van.

This, though, is what the object looked like. If you took curved chrome panels about ten feet high and ten feet wide, each one of slightly different shades, then welded them all together in a shape resembling a tuna fish can—that is what the object looked like. It was rapidly spinning and skimming along just above the tree tops behind the van.

I watched the object for no more than five seconds before I went off the road. When I looked back again the object, or craft, was no longer there. I asked Joy but she had no idea what—or who—it might have been.

Was It Pointless Jargon?

I encountered what I think was the same object about a week later. I was in about the same place on the Boynton Pass Road going in the same direction. It was about the same time of night.

I had a CB radio then in my van and was talking to a man in Jerome. Jerome is ten air miles away from that spot. The man's voice was coming in as if he were a hundred yards away. The voice was very strong. Rather odd, for the fact that Jerome is generally out of CB range in that area. This puzzled me quite a bit at the time. I don't recall exactly what we were talking about but the conversation was really unusual.

I was completely distracted talking to this guy trying to figure out what it was he was trying to say. I drove down into a dip and around a corner in the road and then up a small rise. And there, right above the road to the right was what appeared to be the same chrome-like object. However, this time it had a companion.

Right next to it was a similar object but about half as big. Neither object appeared to be spinning. They didn't seem to be moving at all. They also, in a way, resembled blank black and white TV screens, as they hung there in the air.

At the time I was so engrossed in the confusing rhetoric of the Jerome man, that it took a few seconds for my mind to even comprehend the two chrome-like objects. I came to a quick left bend in the road, lost sight of them, and when I drove around the far side of the turn both objects were no where to be seen. The man on my CB continued to prattle on in that seeming pointless jargon. The whole thing happened so fast, had I not been totally distracted by the Jerome man, I may have been able to stop in the road and perhaps even get a good steady photo of the objects. The whole episode was weird to the max all the way around.

By the way, while you read this book, if you think some of my stories sound crazy and implausible ask around Sedona and you will find plenty of people with stories just like these. I was sitting with a group of friends in a local restaurant the other day and I was simply amazed (and comforted) that so many other people—normal people—have had paranormal experiences just as weird, or weirder, than I've had. I really enjoyed myself listening to those stories. There was a school teacher, an auto mechanic, a store owner, an advertising salesman and a bank clerk—normal people. Although, of course, I have to add that Sedona is in itself in no way a normal place compared to other "normal" cities around the county.

Photo taken near Sedona in 1998 by Spar Giedeman.

CHAPTER TWO

Some Possible Explanations, or— We May Not Be Who We Think We Are

Linda Bradshaw and I were once described on national television as alien hunters and that depiction is probably pretty accurate. Linda and I would, with determination, go looking for these anomalous enigmas, so that may be, simply, why we encountered them so often.

I've exercised my own intuitive inner sources and psychic abilities. I've gone to channels, psychics, contactees, religious types, read a million books and I'm still almost as perplexed by it all as in the beginning, twenty years ago. All paranormal enigmas must have an obvious purpose. Is it, indeed, our job to discover the perpetrator(s)? Is it mine or someone else's (human) subconscious creating the bulk of paranormal phenomena that we experience? I think that's a possibility, but if that's the root of it all then we all have cause for concern for it would mean the human brain is far more powerful than we realize. A loose cannon?

Are paranormal enigmas holograms?

Someone said to me recently, "Could it be that, there are many new souls coming to this planet and they just don't understand or have comprehension? And, is that itself causing great confusion?" Hmmm .... .

Is someone out there playing games with us? Who has the joy stick in their hands? And are (in the end) these games designed to be malevolent? And deadly? Or so loving and compassionate as to be almost incomprehensible at this time? And no, I don't think God is the prime mover. I think he/she is in the background watching intently. I do believe in God whoever she/he may turn out to be. But I think there is an immensely powerful force allowed by Higher Powers to continue these weird earthly games for educational purposes. Ours and theirs. And ultimately I suppose Gods.

Over the last twenty years I have corralled at every opportunity some of the best, brightest, interested, minds on this planet. I'm talking about minds that explore every possibility, not just one or two. As a result I have found that no one—and I mean no one—can get an overall, realistic, consistent, solid grasp on this paranormal phenomena which is going on around us all the time. I'm talking about a rational explanation.

I'm getting into a lot of exploratory possibilities in these early pages for the reason that I want to prime minds for the stories to come. I want to lay some groundwork first. Maybe out there somewhere is someone who will have an idea or a revelation that will crack this whole thing wide open. For me that would be a dream come true.

There are well researched theories that an alien race such as the Reptilians are in all high positions of control in military, government and banking everywhere on this planet. For one, read David Icke's controversial, runaway best seller *The Biggest Secret*. The Reptilian proposition is a stunning idea backed up with some sobering and hard to argue with evidence.

A wide spread report has it that before Princess Diana died (murdered) she confided to close friends that some of the people in control in England "are not human, those people are lizards."

Icke's book (for one) claims that the Reptilians can shape shift and appear physically to us as a male or female human. Or in some cases dominate and manipulate humans mentally from another dimension. Or still further can appear to the governments, the military and the businesses that they control in their natural physical form as a humanoid reptile.

Mind boggling, isn't it. What if it's true?

Incidentally, in my years of doing first hand research on UFO's and aliens I have two or three times run across eerie evidence of Reptilians that would give anyone the creeps. Slim evidence to be sure but it was there. I talked about it in *Merging Dimensions,* and in several of my other books.

I think whatever it is that's really running the show does not normally have a physical form at all. At least not in this dimension. Further on in the book I will talk about an intriguing theory I recently came across. It has to do with time travelers. Time travel(ers) may hold the key, the nucleus, to the entire phenomena.

I think that at least some anomalous phenomena is certainly coming from another dimension. This photo may be evidence of that.

Photo credit: Linda White Eagle

This photo is not a hoax. In fact, I am the one who discovered the creature in the photograph. I was shown some photos of a recent Indian ceremony that the woman in the photo had attended near Sedona. It doesn't show up distinctly in the book reproduction but it seems the (not visible at the time the photo was shot) creature is poking its head through some sort of film-like substance. It almost looks like the creature is under water and poked its head above the surface for a look around. Perhaps it was attracted by the flash of the camera. The body of the creature is rather opaque and indistinct as it would be if it were underwater. Could the water effect be another dimension? Whatever it is, it's a strange creature. It has a nose like a rabbit and eyes like a snake. Endless questions of who or what it might be and where it came from. Disregard the man with the camera to the left of her head and the whited out bushes in the far back ground.

All evidence that I present in any of my writings is the truth as I know it and have seen it. I have been the victim of far too many devious and mindless hoaxes to ever perpetrate one myself. There may be singular cases when to the best of my abilities and intentions I was simply wrong or made a mistake. But never a hoax or fabrication.

Bill Hamilton Saw It Too

In many of the sightings or incidents I have been involved in I had a witness, or witnesses, who were standing near me and saw exactly the same thing that I did. One of these occasions in 1995 involved Bill Hamilton. Bill is a friend of mine. Bill is a man of integrity and is one of the world's most respected UFO researchers. He has been a UFO researcher since about the age of ten. He is in his fifties now. Bill had the honor of being at Giant Rock, California in the 1950's and spent time with the legendary UFO contactee George Van Tassel. Giant Rock was in the southern Mojave Desert and was located near Twenty-nine Palms. Any modern UFO researcher would give almost anything to have spent time with George Van Tassel. I'll tell a story about him shortly.

So Bill and I were standing out in front of the ranch house at the Bradshaw Ranch one summer night in 1995. Naturally we were talking about UFO's, when suddenly an enormous ball of light (it looked like a car headlight on high beam) rose up out of the trees a quarter mile south of where we stood. We stopped talking and intently watched the blazing light.

The light slowly rose up to about five hundred feet above the desert floor, then made a 90 degree turn to the northeast. The light was moving at a speed of about thirty miles per hour. It had not gone far when it abruptly transformed itself into the running light pattern of a single engine aircraft.

There was a steady burning red light, an amber light and a white strobe in the middle. It then flew right over Sedona. Anyone looking up would not have looked twice.

It mimicked a light plane perfectly except that it was silent. At least while we watched it was. It was a once in a lifetime event/sighting for most people.

The whole thing took about ten minutes. I kept expecting Bill to get real excited and jump up and down like a normal person would. After the lights flew almost out of sight Bill casually remarked in an almost indifferent tone, "You know . . . I saw something like that once near the Tehachapi Pass." I thought to myself, "Damn." I guess I'm not the only one to be blase` about these things!

George Van Tassel

Giant Rock, back in the 1950's was the scene of some of the most profound UFO and alien activity which has ever taken place on this planet. (I have recently been told that it is now called Split Rock. This is reportedly the world's largest single boulder and in 1998 it mysteriously split in half. This has caused an enormous amount of conjecture among New Agers, UFO researchers and local Mojave Indian Tribes.) Some of the UFO/alien events at Giant Rock were eyewitnessed by dozens of people. Bill Hamilton was there and so was local resident Bob Short. Bob Short, in his late sixties, is also one of the pioneers of UFO research. I have listened to a number of fascinating Giant Rock stories from these two pioneers. Here is one of the best.

It seems Van Tassel was an early channeler and he used to channel aliens. At any rate, one night at Giant Rock Van Tassel was conducting a channeling session to a room full of people. Right in the middle of the session he suddenly became quiet—as if he were listening to some sort of instructions from an unseen source.

Van Tassel then with no warning leaped to his feet and ran out of the room. He dashed across a dirt airstrip and jumped into his pick-up truck. The crowd of attendees was not far behind him.

Van Tassel drove down the runway (there was a small airstrip then at Giant Rock) and as he did a huge flying saucer descended rapidly out of the clouds. The saucer stopped silently above the runway and a wide door opened and then a ramp came down to the ground. Van Tassel slowed and drove his pick-up right up the ramp and into the ship. The door closed behind Van Tassel's truck and the saucer rose back up into the clouds. A few hours later the saucer brought George Van Tassel and his truck back to the same spot. Evidently he wouldn't talk much about what took place inside the saucer. I'm sure he had his reasons. Dozens of reputable people witnessed the event. From different highly credible sources I've heard many Giant Rock stories like this. Giant Rock, as an establishment however, is no longer there. The whole place was dismantled by someone, military or real estate, I don't remember who, but it must have been an exciting place to be back in the 1950's.

A Dry Creek Sighting

In the summer of 1995 six people (four men, two women) had a dramatic sighting. We were out sky watching one night off Dry Creek Road a few miles from Sedona. About 8:30 p.m. somebody shouted, "Hey, look at that!" We all turned to where he was pointing toward the horizon.

Something was coming in our direction from the western horizon. The sun had just set and it was not yet fully dark. That's probably why we saw the object so well because, at that height, the sun was still shining on it. The object flew at a fantastic speed over us. The thing was so odd looking it is still hard to describe it. It was as shiny as the shiniest chrome and it seemed composed of blocks stuck together like a half dozen sugar cubes stuck together randomly. It was tumbling rapidly as it went over us. It flew horizon to horizon in less than five seconds—at most. It was not a satellite, it was far too close to the earth.

Who Is Really In Charge?

Eight years ago I had one of my coffee shop meetings with an exceedingly intelligent man in his early thirties. He wanted to discuss some things I wrote in a magazine article. We spent a few hours in the coffee shop and it turned out that his father was a man high up in international politics. His father knew most of the world's insiders in banking, politics and the military. These are the people who determine everything that happens on this planet—including wars.

So after I found out about his father I told him what I knew about the so-called Secret World Government. It seems that the Secret World Government was a topic he had researched and was of great concern to him also. Such as the Secret World Government controlling the global population by introducing new no-cure diseases, thereby killing off half the world's population and getting rid of the "useless eaters" as we have been called. And by devious—no choice—means installing a one world government by taking over the world's military, political offices and banking to create a global dictatorship. These are the high points but there is and was much more.

This man's father was at the time a member of the CFR—Council on Foreign Relations. This is an exclusive club (by invitation only) and these people are the elite of world movers and shakers. His father was also connected to the secretive Bilderberger Group and the Club of Rome.

His interest piqued by our talk, he went to see his father at the first opportunity. He relayed to his father what we had discussed. His father said something to him that impressed me deeply. The son later told me that after he had finished expressing this wealth of subversive information to his attentive father, his father looked down at his desk and grew quiet for some moments. He then looked up and said to his son, "You know . . . those people just aren't that smart."

So if this is true, and I'm sure it is, here is where we are with this. Those of us who make a study of the Sinister Secret World Government arena are well aware that somebody invisible to us is indeed controlling, manipulating and confusing just about every aspect of life on this planet. Exclusive of sudden disasters like volcanoes, earthquakes, and solar flares.

If it isn't the CFR, the Bilderbergers, the Illuminati, the Club of Rome, the Trilateral Commission, or the Masons, it means there is someone else. Reptilians perhaps? Time travelers? I doubt that it is the people we see on television. Questions, many questions. It's about time we found out who they are.

In all fairness—I've taken a bit of flak from several learned sources for my comments on the Secret World Government. One source, whom I trust intimately, has spent a good deal of time with several of these lofty factions of world government. He says that these groups have been and are doing everything in their power to improve the over-all condition of humanity on this planet.

Then if not the Trilateral Commission, The Club of Rome, etc. Then I will continue to assert that there is some all powerful hidden group that is raising hell with the struggles of the average human on this planet. There are many who are far more connected than I, who would agree with me on that point. In fact, recently I attended a lecture by one of this countries most noted and respected UFO researchers who is also a medical doctor. During his presentation he remarked that he had been told by someone high in the U.S. government of the following incident. Three people were having a conversation with Bill Clinton and he was alleged to have made the following remark. "We know there is a secret government within the government which is controlling everything, and there is nothing I can do about it."

CHAPTER THREE

The Alien Tunnel System

I once said I would never write about this subject because I thought the subject was simply too dangerous for everyone involved. I have so far only related this following information to my closest, most trusted researcher friends. It is a discussion of the probable alien underground tunnel system in the Flagstaff—Sedona—Clarkdale—Jerome areas. Here, I will relate everything I know about the subject. Ten or twenty years ago people got killed, or scared off from talking about this sort of information. I have lost a few friends. But it seems now there is some sort of hands-off policy because everyone is writing about everything and no one has had any suspicious, sudden accidents for a long time now. At least nothing that I'm aware of.

(Several months before publication of this book, I learned about two threats of bodily harm to anyone pursuing research of underground bases and tunnels in this area. One of the threats came directly from one of Arizona's largest corporations. Proof of the existence of an underground tunnel system?)

This is a deep tunnel system that probably starts at (or is connected to) the Navajo Army Depot near Flagstaff, Arizona. The Navajo Army Depot is thirty miles northwest of Sedona. The Depot is approximately six miles long by five miles wide. The U.S. military has stored munitions there such as bombs, and artillery shells as well as a nuclear arsenal. The nuclear arsenal is played down but it's there.

In 1997 I talked to a Flagstaff man who had been dispatched by his employer to deliver some construction goods to the Navajo Army Depot. This is simply a delivery driver dispatched to make an everyday routine delivery. He drove up to a guard station at the entrance to the depot.

No one was there. Thinking that there must be another guard station further on, he drove on through the open gate.

As he maneuvered a vast network of gravel roads it wasn't long before he realized he was lost. In an opening in the ponderosa pine forest to his left, to his utter astonishment, he found himself staring at an enormous flying saucer sitting on the ground. He said as he drove by the opening, he soon was in total shock. He went on to say that moments later as he drove along military police in vehicles closed in on his truck from all directions.

He remarked that he was scared to death. Because of what he saw he thought he would be shot or spend the rest of his life in some hidden prison.

After he nervously explained his story about why he was there and how he got where he was, they—under armed guard—allowed him to make his delivery and leave. Nothing was asked or said about the huge disc-shaped craft.

If that is a made-up tale it's a good one. I have no way of verifying stories like that. But it fits in very well with the location and other stories with a similar theme I've heard from other people.

I am reasonably certain that unknown alien types are working with the U.S. military in relation to this tunnel system. The delivery driver's experience is one more piece of evidence. I'm assuming that the tunnel system ends at, begins at, or is interconnected with the Navajo Army Depot simply because the depot would be a logical part of the tunnel system.

And it doesn't take a lot of thinking to deduce that the tunnel system must be connected somewhere at some point with a larger network of tunnels. Perhaps stretching across the U.S. or even around the world. And if the tunnel system is exclusive to this area—why is it here? If it is exclusive to this area, then there must be some enormous strategic importance to this place, being Sedona and the surrounding Verde Valley.

From the Navajo Army Depot we continue on south to Secret Canyon. This is a direct line distance of ten miles. From Secret Canyon (six miles long) the tunnel system turns south and continues in a straight line distance of fifteen miles to the mountainside mining town of Jerome. Jerome was established in the 1800's and over a billion dollars worth of copper was taken out of its mine shafts.

Jerome has seventy-seven miles of mostly dry tunnels under its streets. Most of these tunnels are still intact and some of the main tunnels are cavernous. One can imagine what might exist in such a network of tunnels, most of which have been closed off from the surface for over eighty years. One of the deepest shafts goes down over four thousand feet into the earth. When they were hauling out copper ore, about three thousand feet down they hit a huge deposit of gold and silver. A small town could be built in the hole they left a half mile below the surface. Maybe there is.

My own evidence, combined with evidence from a half dozen other local information gatherers, indicates that a "base" probably exists under the town of Jerome and extends back to the nearby town of Clarkdale. I wish I could include some of the rumors I have heard about the town of Jerome and the international high level movers and shakers who have been clandestinely visiting there. But the rumors are too wild even for this book.

Getting back to the canyons, there have been so many gun point encounters in the canyons along the tunnel route that there is not space enough in this book to list them all. There have been at least forty. These are encounters where hikers ran into gun-toting military types guarding something unknown. That something unknown can only be openings down into the underground tunnel system. Those tunnel openings when not in use must be well camouflaged. And when they are in use, to be in the area is a decidedly dangerous affair.

These canyons, in order from north to south, are: Secret Canyon, Long Canyon, Boynton Canyon, Fay Canyon, Red Canyon, and Loy Canyon. Each one of these canyons in the last twelve years has had its share of hiker-military incidents.

In 1989 there were several curious incidents which no doubt lend evidence to the probability of an underground tunnel system.

In 1989 a woman was riding her horse in a remote section of Boynton Canyon and came upon a substantial pile of large metal boxes stencilled with the words U.S. Dept. Of Commerce. The stack of containers was surrounded by a chain link fence to keep people out. About the same time several other hikers came upon the same stash of boxes. Some of these containers were evidently quite large—double refrigerator sized or so. Metal boxes in a remote part of Boynton Canyon labeled U.S. Dept. Of Commerce? An extraordinarily unusual discovery.

Sycamore Canyon

This chapter would not be complete without some mention of Sycamore Canyon. It is said to be thirty-three miles long if one follows all of its curves and bends. It's about fifteen miles long as the crow flies. Deep and wide Sycamore Creek flows through its lower stretches.

Some parts of the canyon are over a mile wide and it runs in a north/south direction. Sycamore Canyon doesn't have the awesome grandeur of Sedona's canyons, it is more of a long valley than a canyon.

It's a long, rough, dusty ride from Clarkdale on a gravel road to reach its mouth. Either that or a long, dusty drive and a long dusty hike to access its mid to upper reaches. Because of its remoteness, I personally have not spent much time there. However, over the years it has been the scene of some extremely strange activities. If there are openings to a tunnel system in Sedona's canyons, then it is 100% likely that there are some in Sycamore Canyon as well.

Sycamore Canyon has been a strange place way back to the time of the Indian wars when Geronimo hid some of his supply caches in Sycamore's caves. Rumor has it that the Spanish discovered a huge deposit of gold high up on the western walls of the canyon. There is evidence that the Apaches wiped out the Spanish and dynamited the mine's entrance flat. Spanish artifacts have been found in that area, although no trace of the mine has been found.

Back in the late 1800's it was a major cattle driving route to Flagstaff. So many cattle got bitten by rattlesnakes that that route was abandoned and another was constructed to the east in Loy Canyon.

It has also been said that Basque sheepherders avoided parts of Sycamore Canyon because strange, giant, hair covered creatures that walked like a man inhabited parts of it. A long standing story has it that a few Basque sheepherders went into Sycamore Canyon—and never came out.

Some of the most unusual paranormal stories I have heard have come out of Sycamore Canyon. I have never had the time to track many of these rumors down. But some people I did track down, and the stories of encounters with alien beings, Bigfoot type creatures, menacing flying craft and general high strangeness stories are among the most dramatic I have ever heard. I can only take note of these stories as I have not spent much time there.

Personally, I don't care for the place—at all. I have been in various parts of Sycamore Canyon on four widely separated occasions. Every time I came out I had an unnamable strange feeling and was in a bad frame of mind. Sycamore Canyon affects a lot of people that way. I have talked to lots of people who have camped and backpacked in Sycamore. They either love the place or hate it. Black and white with no in-between.

Had Sycamore Canyon been frequented by as many people as Sedona's canyons have, I would venture a guess that the most dramatic paranormal events would have taken place there. And may yet in the near future.

Much of the decline of the activity around Sedona is due I think to simply too many people. My bet is that a lot of the activity has re-located to Sycamore Canyon and Sycamores huge side canyons. If so, then the future will be interesting in regard to Sycamore Canyon. It will be many years before it is as accessible as Sedona's canyons are.

Back to the Tunnel System

When the tunnel system, or whatever it actually turns out to be, is open at the surface there is great danger in being in the vicinity of the opening. I need to reiterate, however, that only one in a thousand hikers has ever had a gun point experience in the canyons. This is an infinitesimally small chance. Personally I feel rather safe writing about the tunnel system now as there have been no incidents that I know of in over two years. So—maybe—the tunnel system is now dormant or is staying underground on a permanent basis. Maybe.

Earlier in the book I mentioned time travelers. I found an article in *NEXUS* magazine's April-May 1999 issue (Volume 6, no. 3). The article is entitled "The Wingmakers." The following is an excerpt of an interview from that story. The Wingmakers are time travelers.

Dr. Anderson: *Cloaking technology is not just science fiction concept. It's been developed for more than 10 years. It's used much more frequently than people realize. And I'm not talking about its diluted version of stealth technology. I'm talking about the ability to superimpose a reality construction over an existing reality that is desired to be hidden.*

For instance, you could walk right up to the entrance of the (deleted) site and see nothing that would look like an entrance or opening. To the observer, it would be a flat wall of rock. And it would have all the characteristics of rock—texture, hardness, and so forth—but it's actually a reality construction that is superimposed on the mind of the observer. In reality, the entrance is there, but it can't be observed because the mind has been duped into the projected reality construction.

That is the best possible definition that I have seen so far that I could apply to the canyon tunnel system.

When hikers (it's always hikers) run into these military types the "soldiers" are either outfitted in camouflage, all black or (believe it or not) fluorescent orange clothing or uniforms. I checked with active military personnel. All of those outfits are in current use by the U.S. military. In the usual gun point scenario there is a surprise encounter by a hiker or hikers with the military types. The military types are not patriot militia or survivalists in training. That possibility was eliminated long ago.

A machine gun, usually an M-16 (or in some cases semi-automatic pistols) is then leveled at the hikers. By the tone of voice of the "soldiers" the hiker(s) is left with no doubt that he will be shot on the spot if he does not turn around, retrace his steps, and rapidly leave the area. As far as I know these hiker incidents have only involved males.

Ninety-nine percent of the tunnel zone is within the boundaries of either the Coconino National Forest or the Prescott National Forest—public property. In a number of the gun point cases I am referring to here I am relying on information supplied to me by reliable researchers. In at least three incidents the gun-in-the-nose-pointee came back angrily with, "This is public land! I'm not turning back! Who the hell are you guys!?"

At that juncture the incident quickly escalated and the pointee wisely left the area in great haste. I know of one incident where the hiker was ready to fight and came within seconds of being shot—or never being heard from again.

Another incident, referred to me by a highly reliable source, was that of two off-duty police officers. These two officers evidently ran into several of these camo types in uniform. The officers were hiking along the lofty saddle which divides Loy Canyon and Secret Mountain. The officers were informed that they were in a military restricted area and to leave the way they came at once. After trekking six miles, the policemen weren't too happy about the prospect of turning back, just as they were about to reach their destination on Secret Mountain. Their reply was, "We are police officers, we aren't going anywhere but in that direction!" as they pointed up the trail. The flat tone answer was, "We have jurisdiction here!" The M-16's leveled in the officers' direction no doubt convinced them not to push the issue further. As with all the others, they turned around and went home.

It's sort of interesting how these things play themselves out. I had some friends who were ex-military officers and intelligence agents who went looking for these mysterious soldier types. They went heavily armed with the intention of aggressively interviewing the soldier types and if it came to it—engage in a shoot-out. At least that was what was said to me. If push came to shove I think they would have condescended like everybody else. Even though some mild attempts at search and contact were made in Secret Canyon, no confrontation ever occurred that I know of. It certainly would have been interesting what retired military intelligence people would have found out. They, for sure, would have asked the right questions.

Gun point incidents are extremely random at best, anyway. So their chances of running into these guards/military/soldier types would have been one in a thousand. Probably.

There have been at least two incidents when a night hiker was targeted with a laser gunsight and warned out of the tunnel area. Both happened in the early 1990's. One incident happened in Long Canyon and the other happened in Secret Canyon. Both incidents were nearly identical in how they transpired. And, I am absolutely certain that both of these incidents have something to do with the probable underground tunnel system.

The Secret Canyon incident involved a colleague of Bill Hamilton. Bill thoroughly investigated this incident. It is one of the most detailed and completely investigated hiker-military incidents that has taken place in this area.

One night this friend of Bill's—I'll call him Robert—was out driving around by himself on the Vultee Arch road doing some UFO sky watching. Robert was near the parking area for the Secret Canyon trailhead when he heard the sounds of idling helicopters on the ground. He parked his car and out of curiosity began walking toward the helicopter sounds.

I have to assume he was on the Secret Canyon trail, for that is the primary way to get into Secret Canyon from the Vultee Arch road. As he got closer to the idling helicopter rotors a voice amplified by a loudspeaker suddenly boomed out of the darkness ahead. The male voice was warning him that he was in a restricted military area (Coconino National Forest) and to return the way he had come.

Robert thought this was a pretty good joke, so he kept on towards the helicopter sounds. Not long after, he looked down at an illuminated red dot that was moving around on his chest. Robert knew instantly that it was a laser gun sight. The booming voice from the bushes asked Robert if he knew what the red dot was. And, if Robert took one more step he would be shot in his tracks. Robert did like everyone else and high-tailed it. Wise move. The next day a big Huey military helicopter followed Robert and his wife all the way to Williams, a distance of over fifty highway miles from Sedona.

Every single one of these gunpoint encounters has taken place along the route of the probable tunnel system. Questions, questions. What is it in those tunnel openings, or whatever in reality it may turn out to be, that "they" are more than ready and willing to kill people over it if need be. I for one would sure as hell like to see it, to know what the "it" is."

Maybe what's in those tunnels would turn out to be something right out of a *Star Wars* movie. Who knows? Somebody knows. How about this: what if those soldier types are not the U.S. military at all but some sort of time travelers, aliens, or interdimensional beings who have their own agenda operating out there in the canyons. Might be the government has been warned off too, or is itself trying to find out what is going on out there in the canyons. The canyon/tunnel/soldier activity has been dormant for years but you can bet it's still going on—on some level.

As an aside to this, in the ten years I have been cautiously writing and talking about the gun point incidents in the canyons I was for a while afraid it would seriously scare tourists and hikers away from the canyon lands. Tourism is a colossal chamber of commerce business around here. But the reaction, instead, of fear has generally been curiosity. I know of only two or three accounts where people were actually scared off from hiking in the canyons resulting from what I wrote.

No doubt every single thing we do is ultimately designed for our personal—and spiritual—growth. No matter what form it takes.

More Canyon Incidents

In one of the more unique incidents in 1994, two out of town hikers and a long-time local wilderness tour guide had gone into Secret Canyon to spend the night. It was early spring and a light rain had by 3:00 a.m. turned into a moderate snowstorm. Deciding that they had better walk out while they still could, they quickly packed their gear and started on the arduous five mile hike back to their cars.

They had not gone far when they saw more flashlights ahead of them on the winding, hilly trail. Logically assuming that the flashlights were more campers trying to get out of the deep canyon, they hurried to catch up with the flashlights.

When they caught up to the men holding the flashlights, they were surprised to see that the four men were dressed in all black ninja-like uniforms with no insignia on the uniforms. The men dressed in black were also more than a bit surprised to see the campers. Then the campers noticed that the men in black were carrying automatic weapons. I believe it would make me a touch nervous if I found myself in that sort of situation at 3:00 a.m. in a snowstorm far back in a remote canyon. The men in black told the astonished campers that they were in a restricted military area and had to vacate the area on the double.

The local tour guide and the two out-of-towners were then marched—at gunpoint—out of Secret Canyon all the way back to their cars. What further stunned them was that a military helicopter appeared at the mouth of Secret Canyon and hovered over the line of men right up until the campers got into their cars and drove away. There have been at least four incidents locally where military helicopters were involved in this manner. Why helicopters?! I don't know what transpired in the way of conversation on the very long walk out of Secret Canyon, but it scared the hell out of the tour guide. He has since moved out of the area, but while here he absolutely refused to discuss the incident. I found out about the details of the incident in a round about way, from one of his friends.

I've said many times that there is scant money in the researching of the paranormal. However, it is anything but a boring business. I had just completed the second re-write of this book when a local (former) tour guide business owner who I was talking to told me of a Secret Canyon incident in which he had first hand knowledge.

I had once known about this incident but had long since forgotten it. In 1992 the mouth of Secret Canyon was cordoned off by military soldiers for two to three days. No one was allowed to go in there. The hikers were, as usual, told that it was a restricted area and military exercises were in operation in Secret Canyon. I've been in Secret Canyon. It's the last place on earth where military exercises might be or should be going on. What was it—really—that the "military" didn't want people to see?

A somewhat similar incident occurred in adjacent Sterling Canyon in 1991 or 1992. However, this time the soldiers on guard were cordial and friendly to the hikers. A lot of conversation took place but the hikers were not told what sort of exercises were going on in Sterling Canyon. An even more unlikely spot for military exercises than even Secret Canyon. The hikers were told by the soldiers that they were U.S. Marines on orders to block the mouth of the canyon. Evidently the marines did not even know for sure what was going on in Sterling Canyon.

David Miller

This is yet another story inserted just weeks before this book was printed. The more I research this story the more it disturbs me. At first I regarded it as a rather run-of-the-mill lost person case, but after digging deeper I am not so sure. You will see what I mean.

On May 22nd, 1988 David Barclay Miller, a forest service ranger stationed at Beaver Creek Ranger Station near Sedona, walked into Secret Canyon and never came out. Miller, then twenty-two years old, was a former resident of Bethesda, Maryland. He was hired by the forest service after college and had been stationed in Sedona for about two months before his disappearance.

While doing research on this story, I discovered that David Miller was an experienced wilderness backpacker. He had climbed to Mt. Rainier's lofty and icy peak, had explored Alaska's mountainous regions with their glacial crevasses and at age thirteen had kayaked along the rocky Maine coast. He had excelled at athletics in high school at Potomac School in McLean, Maryland. He was a young man in superb physical condition.

Miller had signed in at the Vultee Arch trailhead on May 22, 1988. He had three days off and when he didn't return on time, a massive search was launched to look for him.

Search parties from the Coconino County Sheriff's Department, the U.S. Forest Service, and several Yavapai County dog search teams and the Yavapai County Sheriff's office mounted search team spent four days looking for Miller. They were joined by the Arizona Department of Public Safety which did an extensive air search. Not a single trace of David Miller was ever found. True, he may have fallen into one of the areas many small and large side canyons. It may be years until some trace of him is discovered, but why didn't the dog teams find him? That area is not that inaccessible. In past years I have been all over it. Miller was the type of athlete who would explore areas a less experienced hiker would not. He was known for that. David was well known for pushing the limits. I know these types of people well. I've spent my whole life around and with them. They go beyond. My question is—did David Miller find or see something he was not supposed to? Anyone having any new or further information on David Miller can write to me at the address at the back of this book.

An Angry State Employee

There might be somewhat of a clue to the happenings in Secret Canyon in this next incident/encounter. In 1993 an Arizona state employee was hiking alone in Secret Canyon. He said he was walking around a house sized boulder and evidently came face to face with an alien creature that was around nine feet tall. This was in the same general area where the tour guide and the two hikers had been camped when it started snowing.

The man told how the alien was wearing some sort of bluish colored uniform. He also said the alien had grey skin, a lightbulb shaped head with huge almond shaped eyes, and did not move at all—it just stared back at him.

The man, scared out of his mind, ran the five or six miles to his car. The reason I heard of this story is that evidently the state employee raised a lot of dust with local and state police and the forest service trying to find out who the humanoid creature was. And, in loud tones demanded an investigation. After a few weeks he was told to keep his mouth shut or he would lose his job—and a lot more.

An Army Intelligence Agent

Ten years ago I had a day long conversation (it was entirely about UFO's and aliens) with a man who was a retired army intelligence agent. While he was in intelligence he said that there were rumors going around in intelligence circles that special units of the army were doing some disturbingly strange things in Secret Canyon.

In fact, he added, one of the agent operatives in an army unit would not go along with what was being done and "they take care of their own." Meaning they killed the guy. Accidents happen.

If this is indeed not just a rumor then it was just one more example that, for a while at least, something of an incredible magnitude was going on in Secret Canyon.

The Secret Mountain Fire

On July 29`, 1994 a forest fire of extremely suspicious origin broke out on the top of Secret Mountain. The fire called the "Lost Fire" burned for five days before any attempt was made to put it out. The fire eventually burned 1800 acres and was put out by rain on August 8`. At the height of the blaze helicopters and UFO's were seen over Secret Mountain. Occasionally yellow smoke was seen billowing off Secret Mountain. Forest fires do not burn yellow. They burn white, grey or black. Since the fire on Secret Mountain there have been no reports of UFO activity there when it was once the hotspot of UFO activity in Northern Arizona. Wonder what really burned—and was it somehow connected with the tunnel system which would be directly under Secret Mountain?

So now we move out of the canyons onto the flat desert heading towards Clarkdale and Jerome following the probable route of the tunnel system. As recently as the summer of 1995 deep underground drilling activity could be clearly heard out in the flat desert. In fact, the underground boring sounds got to be extremely annoying to some of the residents who lived in the area. Telephone poles shook and vibrated, wires swayed back and forth, water pipes vibrated noisily and a heavy drilling sound could at times be clearly heard above ground.

How deep the drilling activity was is hard to ascertain, but a good guess would be three hundred feet or so down. These boring sounds were present for a month or so, then gradually faded in the direction of Jerome.

From a scientific friend in Illinois, I obtained a sophisticated hydrophone device that when attached to a tape recorder is extremely effective in recording deep underground sounds. The very week I obtained this device the underground boring sounds stopped. I never got a chance to use it.

It's long been known that machines that can bore a tunnel up to fifty feet in diameter have been in use in this country. In use mostly by the government. These are machines that either chew a tunnel through solid rock or are automated machines that are nuclear powered and literally melt the rock as they go along. The molten rock is then funneled toward the rear of the machine and disposed of. The walls of the tunnel are left as smooth as glass after this process.

For those who are interested, read the excellent well researched books written by Richard Sauder, Ph.D. Dr. Sauder is one of the world's leading experts on underground tunnels and bases, and is an honest man.

The Peck's Lake Incident

Across the desert, following the tunnel route, we come to Peck's Lake on the outskirts of the small town of Clarkdale. Peck's Lake is a horseshoe shaped pond about a half mile long created for the recreational use of the 1800's copper miners.

Before I go into detail, I will mention that I got this story from three different sources who all told it in exactly the same way. One of these sources is a former CIA agent.

As I understand it, two off-duty policemen were hiking north of Peck's Lake and to their great surprise happened on to a manhole with the cover off to one side. This is the same type of manhole one would find in any city. The area the two men were in is a hot, flat, open, and sandy desert. There was a ladder going down into the hole. After some conversation they decided to climb down into the hole to see what was there. I have a feeling they probably thought the manhole had something to do with drug smuggling and I don't know if the two men were armed.

At the bottom of the ladder they found themselves in a labyrinth of tunnels going in a variety of directions. Suddenly, "military came swarming out of the tunnels like rats!" said one of the officers. The officers weren't evidently harmed in any way but were abruptly told to take a walk and forget what they found.

Several months later, in the company of a Phoenix UFO researcher, I walked that same general area on a 108 degree day. If a manhole was in that area a dead cactus or bush or a couple of shovels of dirt could be thrown on top of it and it would never be seen. It would take a small army weeks to find it just poking and digging around. A good guess is that the covers are a heavy plastic. In that event finding them with electronic equipment like a metal detector would be difficult if not impossible.

At this point, for those of you who are wondering—I do not reveal my sources. Unless it simply doesn't matter either way. I've mentioned this before in several of my other books. There are various reasons for not talking about sources. But the main reason is that some people could get harmed in a variety of ways. For close trusted researchers I will reveal almost everything I know about a particular person or subject or event. In other words, I have the evidence to support what I write about.

Experiencers will often come to me when they will not talk to other researchers. It is well known that I will not publicly expose sources. I would have a hard time living with myself if someone's life was ruined over something I wrote which involved that person.

I know that isn't a very journalistic approach but that's the way it is. I read books where the author gives the name, date, place and the life story of each of his or her sources. If I did that few experiencers of significance would talk to me.

Here is a dramatic example of a clandestine meeting I had with a man and his wife in 1994. I never knew their names. I didn't ask and they didn't tell me. This is a long story and I'm going to greatly condense it here. In short, when the man was a small boy of five his father smuggled him into a military base in a pick-up truck. His father had a top secret clearance. The father wanted his son to see what was there. For the future I suppose.

The father got out. He told the boy to stay out of sight in the truck. The little boy hid in the pick-up under some large articles on the front seat. On the base four completely different sirens went off one after the other and when they stopped the little boy peeked out the truck window. There was not a human being in sight on this large western state base. As the boy watched, out of the ground slowly rose an enormous disc-shaped craft. It was sitting on an elevator. He said the ship was about three hundred feet in diameter. The huge disc was then guided automatically into an enormous aircraft hanger. This was in 1955. Base security guards did not detect the boy.

The boy used to play in his father's office when his father was away at work. When he was about ten the boy stole a folder out of his father's filing cabinet. It was all about aliens—photos and all. That is why the boy took the file. He liked the cute and odd little human-like creatures in the black and white photos. Most of whom he said were dead. The aliens were lying in various positions as if they had died in some sort of explosion—or crash. The aliens did not all look exactly alike, he explained. He said he thought that three different races were depicted in the photos. He did say that one type of alien was so human looking they could walk down a street and no one would look twice. They looked much like human children.

I tried all sorts of cajoling just to get a look at that file folder. I didn't ask to copy or photograph anything—just look. After that day I never heard from or saw the man again. Maybe he didn't trust me, or he was a government man trying to feel me out, or maybe he thought I knew something. As far as I know that folder has never surfaced. If that folder really existed (and I think it does) there were and are titanic risks involved with it all around.

This is a strange life we lead, here on planet Earth.

He Almost Pushed It Too Far

This last tunnel related incident was one that I was directly, and personally involved in. I spent a good bit of time interviewing the two researchers involved. It is two separate incidents that happened in the same place. And it's a rather unnerving story, which is one of the reasons I have not pursued this whole tunnel enigma more than just noting available information that falls into my lap.

Both of these fellows had a similar experience in exactly the same area. I will call them Paul and Daniel.

Paul had recently been discharged from the U.S. Air Force (honorably). He had at one time been a serious candidate for air force intelligence school. So he knew what he was talking about, particularly from a military standpoint. Paul is a local underground base researcher and UFO buff. He had been actively following the rumors of a secret underground installation of some sort in the Clarkdale area.

He had focused his efforts on a pinpointed area in the general vicinity of the old power plant on the Verde River north of Clarkdale. And for many reasons I'm not going to say precisely where that spot is.

It was a hot early summer day when Paul began his hike. It was 10:17 a.m. on July 1, 1997. I'm still not sure why he chose that specific area in the first place. He never told me the reason why he wanted to go there. But it is the most unlikely place anyone would ever—and I mean ever—go for a hike. Fun or otherwise. As I later discovered Paul and Daniel had their experiences in precisely the same small spot. Daniel never told me exactly why he chose that area either.

Paul had gone a fair distance when he heard the racing engine sounds of vehicles fast coming in his direction. Curious, he turned to look and two military Humvees were headed in his direction. Paul watched as the two Humvees stopped a hundred yards or so away. Two men dressed in military camouflage uniforms got out. They were carrying rifles he recognized as M-16's. One of the young military drivers began shouting something to Paul. The uniformed man was saying that Paul was in a restricted area. The reason was that military exercises were going on nearby and it could be dangerous. Military exercises!? Paul thought. Here!?

Curious and somewhat irritated, he made his way to where the two men were waiting. As Paul neared the two uniformed men he carefully scrutinized the entire scene. He saw that the two men were dressed in standard lace-up military boots and wore camo uniforms with no insignia except for a black plastic badge over the left shirt pocket. The black badge had small white lettering on it. Both men had 9mm sidearms in hip holsters. The Humvees had camouflage paint and had no license plates or other identifiable insignia on them.

The "military" men repeated what they had earlier said and politely asked Paul to leave the area. Paul didn't budge, but instead began to ask some pointed questions of his own as to why the two men were there in that place. He was asking fundamental questions drawn from his Air Force experience. He said that the two uniformed men began to get visibly nervous.

Paul told me that just about that time the roar of approaching helicopters became plainly audible. Two Vietnam era combat UH-1 helicopters (Hueys) came skimming over a nearby hill. One Huey hovered directly above the three men and the second Huey flew in wide circles around the area. As Paul watched the two helicopters, he told me what was really strange was that the Hueys were a bright silver color, not black or the usual drab olive-green. This is highly unusual.

Paul remarked that at that point, by the escalating seriousness of the situation, he had no doubts that he would be shot or hauled off if he did not stop asking questions and leave. He wisely made a hasty retreat back to his waiting car. That was the end of the matter. He was not approached later.

As it turns out another man from Clarkdale may not have been so fortunate as Paul. In the summer of 1992 this Clarkdale man went for a walk in the same general area that Paul and Daniel had been in. I was told the man has not been seen since. True, the man may have simply gotten into a car and driven away to a new life somewhere, but he

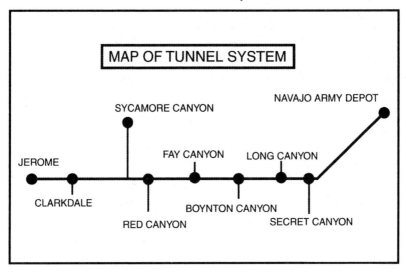

reportedly had a family, a job and he has not been seen since. A friend of mine interviewed the missing man's family. A connection there, perhaps? To Paul and Daniel's encounters?

Transylvania

A quarter mile from Clarkdale to the west is a fifty or so acre tract of land with several very large buildings on it. One of these large buildings was once the smelter for the enormous amounts of copper ore that were brought out of the mines in Jerome. The place is officially called Transylvania. Rumors have swirled around this abandoned place for years. Most of the rumors can not be substantiated in any provable way, but it is near Clarkdale and below Jerome and is near to the strangest "military" activity in the area. Many UFO sightings have been reported in that area over the years also. So the place has to be suspect. It is surrounded by a chain link fence with barbed wire on top.

There is a large sign which reads Transylvania over the main entrance. I was told by locals that the last name of the man who now owns the property is—Transylvania. True or not that makes for some stimulating conversation.

There was for some months three white busses with the windows blacked out parked in the middle of the Transylvania property. On the top of the busses was what could have been air conditioning units. Why would white painted busses with the windows painted black be parked on an old ore smelting property? I saw these myself.

Then There Was Daniel

Daniel is a long time friend of mine and he is the one who did the in-depth investigation on the missing Clarkdale man. Several years previously Daniel had an experience very similar to Paul's in the same location. Daniel has the uncanny knack of getting into trouble poking around areas of unusual activity where a normal person would not normally be drawn to. Daniel told me that he was walking around in the same area that Paul had been in. He said that suddenly two men stepped in front of him from behind some boulders. He added that the two men were dressed like miners. They were carrying high powered deer rifles. Deliverance? M16's would have been a trifle suspicious.

Daniel remarked as how the two men were mean as hell. They told Daniel he was trespassing on private property and to hustle his ass out of there in a hurry.

It is not private property—I checked. Like everybody else, Daniel left in a hurry.

As a footnote to this, a few months after Paul's narrow escape Daniel and I were at a restaurant in Camp Verde. We were discussing some extremely clandestine information we had just heard. Camp Verde is fifteen miles east of Clarkdale. We ran into one of those guys that Paul had described. Lace-up military boots, camo uniform and a black plastic badge with white lettering on it. I noticed right away that the black badge could be removed in seconds. He had sergeant stripes on his arms that were barely visible as they were camo also. He passed us without a word or a look.

I find it interesting that some people won't read my books because they say they are too scary. They always use that word. These things I write about are reality, and unless a number of us at least give them a good hearing, this scary is going to rear up some day and give us a sucker punch. None of it is scary if it is dealt with straight on. Rationally.

Two new domes at the Phoenix Cement plant, Clarkdale, Arizona.

CHAPTER FOUR

Back At The Ranch

I will now relate some more of the events which occurred at the Bradshaw Ranch shortly after *Merging Dimensions* was completed. I must re-emphasize again that as outlandish and bizarre as many of the following stories sound, they are precisely as were witnessed by myself and Linda Bradshaw. In some cases there were eye-witnesses along with Linda and myself.

A case in point is the following incident that took place in mid-summer 1996. It was about 10:00 p.m. and it had been a quiet evening of taking photos trying to capture something on film. Present were Linda, myself and Kim Hormel. Kim was an interested observer in the strange goings-on at the ranch. She was a research participant on a number of occasions at the ranch.

I had walked back to my van to get more film, as I was running low and needed to change the roll in the camera. I was about seventy-five feet from Kim and Linda when all seven of the ranch dogs leaped to their feet in unison. They were barking savagely as they charged full speed past the two women (the Bradshaw's took in stray or abandoned dogs that wandered onto the ranch—hence seven dogs). At about that moment Linda and Kim turned their powerful six volt flashlights in the direction that the dogs were running. They were trying to see what got the dogs so stirred up.

The two powerful beams of light fell on a "man" walking rapidly in a diagonal direction away from us. He did not once look back at us but kept his face away so that we could not see it.

As he hurried by a yucca plant, I gauged his height to be approximately five feet five inches and his weight (in human terms) to be about one hundred and fifty pounds. This "man" was a light tan color from the top of his head to the bottom of his shoes. He had a full head of hair. Everything was that sandy brown color; shoes, hair, skin, clothes, hands—everything.

He was about a hundred and fifty feet away from me and about half that distance from Kim and Linda. The racing dogs caught up to the man and in an instant he simply disappeared—vanished into thin air.

The dogs milled around the spot for awhile and then casually ambled back to their sleeping places near me. We know the man was not a figment of our imagination because the dogs attacked him. Until the dogs started running we had not a hint that anything was out of the ordinary. How long and how often had "he" been there watching us?

The next day about noon we went to the same ground the man had traveled across the night before. We had not disturbed the area of the night before. The ground there was powder dry and a normal foot print sunk in two inches because the soil was so soft.

To our utter surprise the "man" had left no footprints whatever. But there were plenty of dog tracks going in all directions. We remembered precisely where the "man" had vanished. For days after we tried experiments like extending our arms through an imaginary opening and easing half-body into this opening we supposed was there. Half-body so we could get back out just in case one or both of us started to disappear.

We surmised that the man must have slipped through some sort of dimensional opening—or portal of some sort. We even tossed rocks and sticks at the spot to see if one of them might disappear. We shot three or four rolls of film in and around that spot. Absolutely nothing unusual happened to us and nothing unusual showed up on film.

If it was a portal of some sort he/it must have opened it and closed it in milliseconds. Or, the man may simply have changed his density so that he became invisible to our eyes—and the dogs. He may have been still there just yards away watching us. You should have been there, I wish you were. I wish a hundred people could have seen it as witnesses. Likewise this next incident.

The Creature From The Unknown

If that last encounter wasn't strange enough then this next incident tops it by five miles. That same summer, a few months after the tan man event, Linda and I were out one night doing what we usually did—taking random flash photos in any direction to see if we could catch anything invisible (to our eyes) on film.

The same seven dogs were either asleep in various personal places or were following us around hoping for some affection—or a small dog treat we always had in our pockets. They were good dogs, except for Jackson. Jackson was a stray mongrel and had unpredictable, sometimes mean moods. A street dog. Then there was Patches. Patches was my favorite, a lovable big black and white teddy bear dog of multiple lineages. But . . . Patches died mysteriously the following summer after the ranch was sprayed from the air with some unknown strong smelling chemical substance. Several of their horses developed serious tumors. Sedona itself has been sprayed at least four times. I had severe lung problems after one of these sprayings. Lung problems are one result of these sprayings.

At the time of this writing, five years after the Bradshaw Ranch spraying, this spraying activity is becoming a national incident. It is now known that U.S. Air Force Boeing KC-135's and KC-10's are being used to spray antibiotic resistant bacteria and pesticides on U.S. citizens. Areas in twenty-two states have been sprayed along with areas in England, Canada, Australia and several other countries.

It will be interesting to see where this goes. The planes being used are painted white or black and some are painted orange on the bottom half. They have no numbers or markings on them.

That night Linda and I spent a good part of our time playing with the dogs and were chatting and taking random flash photos at the same time. I remember that it was a beautiful night. High desert nights in the summer are simply marvelous, since they are usually dry, fragrant, and comfortable.

Suddenly, demanding our attention, we heard a distinctly odd sound to our left from the far side of the Bradshaw's small fruit orchard. It was a sort of grunting sound and it seemed to be about seventy-five yards away. Some of the sleeping dogs raised their heads at the sound and the ones standing or sitting turned and looked in that direction.

Linda and I were not right then alarmed. We casually discussed what the sound might have been. A mountain lion? A bear? Javalina? Wild dog? Deer? Horse or a cow? None of those possibilities fit the nature of the sound. Then the grunting sound came again. A bit louder and it was then apparent that whatever it was was moving in an arc around us and away from us.

The strange grunts came several more times. They got louder each time and whatever the creature was it was still moving away. The night was pitch dark. Then came a sound that riveted both Linda and myself.

The sound was a cross between a grunt and a roar. Heavy and loud. At once it reminded me of an African lion I once heard roar in a small Florida zoo. A lion's roar can be heard for miles. This was almost that loud.

The dogs all spontaneously went racing off in the direction of the roar. I turned to Linda (amongst a flurry of four letter words) and said that I guessed the creature must weigh at least a thousand pounds to make a sound like that. We both thought it was a Bigfoot.

I thought the next sounds we would hear would be the sounds of dogs being torn to pieces in the distance. What would, or could we do then, I thought to myself. But the dogs never made any sound—nothing. Not even a whimper. Then about ten minutes later the dogs all came ambling back totally at ease and settled back down again. Even Jackson—and Jackson would attack anything. The dogs knew the creature! They were comfortably familiar with it!

Had it been any sort of wild animal like a mountain lion, or a bear, there would have been a horrendous fight, or at a minimum at least chase sounds.

But nothing. The dogs knew the creature well and surely must have interacted with it before. The dogs were free to roam the ranch most all of the time.

But conversely, radically conversely, there were at the time two horse corrals on the ranch. One at the north and one to the southeast. They were about three hundred yards apart. There were two horses in the south corral and two or three in the north corral.

The creature didn't faze the dogs an iota, but the creature made the horses crazy. And I mean crazy. Plenty of tangible proof we weren't imagining the whole experience. The horses were literally screaming. If you have never heard a horse scream, it is a wildly unnerving experience. Believe me. We could hear the pounding of horse hooves as the horses ran back and forth in their corrals. Occasionally one would resoundingly kick the corral boards with its hooves.

We could also hear the creature moving toward the south corral and the two trapped horses. We stood there in the pitch dark night feeling small and helpless. We finally got up the courage to try to find out what the creature was. We couldn't just stand there. Linda and I both have an aggressive, consuming curiosity anyhow.

At the time we both had million and a half candlepower portable spotlights which we took with us. We had been saving mine, as Linda's was by then eighty percent discharged. We walked slowly, step-by-step, over a hundred yards in the direction of the south corral. We stopped about thirty yards away from a cluster of twenty foot tall Arizona alders.

I had concluded that the creature must have been inside the cluster of sapling alders—but it wasn't. There was a long open ridge behind and slightly above the alders, and that's where the creature was. Just its head was above the ridge as it watched us. We found that out the next day.

The horses by then had settled down. Linda and I were losing our nerve in the darkness, especially now that my spotlight was losing power and was growing dimmer by the minute. We decided to go back to the ranch house to safety. We also realized that if whatever it was out there attacked us suddenly, we probably wouldn't stand a chance. Linda Bradshaw is one of the most intelligent, toughest and level-headed people I've ever known. She didn't once complain and didn't show uncontrolled emotion out there in the middle of that dark field. I was more than a bit scared and I'm sure she was too. It was one of the few times that I felt that I was in a situation that was out of any kind of reasonable control. In a high strangeness encounter like that one feels puny, insignificant, totally impotent.

The following day, in nice, bright, safe sunshine we thoroughly examined the area of the encounter of the night before. On the other side of the long ridge we found the creatures' tracks. They were five toed, round and huge. I have big hands and I could put one outstretched hand completely inside one of the tracks. The tracks, I counted twenty-three in all, were of a bipedal creature. The footprints were 36 to 48 inches apart. I am six foot three and my walking stride is 24 inches heel to toe. This would make the two legged creature at least ten feet tall.

Linda and I staked out the tracks with wooden 2 X 2's and then photographed the stakes and the tracks. In two of the tracks deep skin creases can clearly be seen. This is quite typical and very significant of huge, hairy creature type footprints. The skin folds are important evidence.

The tracks were several inches deep in the semi-hard soil indicating a probable weight of around a thousand pounds. A bipedal animal expert might disagree with me but those are my conclusions. That night—in all the confusion—had I thought to grab my night vision binoculars which were right there in my van—in all likelihood we would have clearly seen the creature's head over the crest of the long ridge.

For over a year I couldn't get the round tracks out of my mind. Perfectly round tracks just didn't make any sense. Then one day I realized that the creature had been walking on its tip-toes (the balls of its feet) as it peered over the top of the ridge at us. If that were the case then the whole foot would have probably been 22 inches or more in length. This is clear evidence that this was not a dangerous or harmful creature. Otherwise it would not have taken such care not to be seen by Linda and myself. In fact this particularly huge creature may have been very timid and gentle. The dogs were not frightened of it or by it.

The line of tracks had come out of a rocky, dry stream bed that curved around the ranch and then the tracks went back down into the stream bed. It was impossible to track either up or down the creek bed. I spent the better part of a whole day trying to find either where the creature originally came into, or finally left the stream bed. I found neither exit or entry points.

It was precisely this time that Linda and I were almost desperately trying to get financial, technical and qualified manpower help. I said qualified because at the time we could have gotten literally hundreds of curious onlooker type "help." This we didn't need or want in any form.

If Linda and Bob had thrown open the gates to the Bradshaw Ranch, they would have had a mass of people camping all over and around the ranch with drugs, booze, fires, kids, barking dogs, cameras and tripods, and loud music. And concession stands. It came close to this several times. You would not believe the entrepreneurial propositions the Bradshaws received during this time. Their patience got stretched, at times, to the limit. Exploitation is an unfortunate side effect of a paranormal event.

It seemed though that few investors were seriously interested in our research. A few were only interested in how much money they could make, and nothing more. And we had plenty of proof in the way of photographs and eye witnesses. Still, no serious takers.

Linda and I gave it our best shot until we were "drained" both financially and mentally. A once in a lifetime opportunity—perhaps an epoch—was missed. I've brought this up again because it was indeed an unspeakable tragedy. Had we had credible scientists with us and better finances and better equipment—what might have been learned? I still get angry when I talk about this.

It's interesting, and perplexing, to note that during that particular time period the BBC, Fox and several cable television documentary crews were, for a few hours, on the ranch. The Paranormal Borderline audio-video crew in just one hour of filming got some astounding flying object footage that was seen by viewers around the world. This was the same crew that shot almost all of the long-running "Sightings" television series. They said that what they saw and filmed in one night on the Bradshaw Ranch topped everything they had ever seen before. This is no small statement.

Even out of this there was zero interest in scientific, well-funded study of the paranormal events on the Bradshaw Ranch. Linda and I thought that at the least someone would come forward and minimally fund our research. Nope. When network TV crews were on the ranch we tried to convince them to leave one of their $50,000 beta-cam cameras with us for even a week. We said we would give them an exclusive on what we filmed. The crews talked to the network bosses. No go.

They can pay an actress one million dollars per episode to star in a mindless weekly TV sitcom. But finance something solid, for pennies to them, that could change the world. We had the proof.

At the time of this writing, the summer of 1999, I, the author, have been on national and worldwide television over twenty-five times counting re-runs too. All done for free. Have I sold a million books? No.

I did these interviews free (included was all of my research material) with the hope of selling enough books to recoup my expenses and/or finance serious research myself. I got tremendous exposure for my books. In all I sold maybe five hundred books more than usual out of all this.

This free advertising would have cost me at least fifty thousand dollars. I tell this to marketing professionals and they look back at me with the blankest, deadpan stare one could imagine. The whole, entire affair was a bottomless enigma.

The paranormal activity that was centered on the Bradshaw Ranch seems to have left. Or has moved away. The activity ceased about 1998. A number of experienced paranormal researchers including Spar Giedeman and Cheryl Dryfka have come up empty-handed out there. That's not to say the activity won't re-emerge full bore someday. Because it might—that's the way of paranormal activity.

Photo taken in 1998 near Sedona by Cheryl Dryfka.

CHAPTER FIVE

Another Strange Incident of the Two-Legged Kind

In the summer of 1996, during a period of ultra-high strangeness in our area of research, I decided to walk the south end of the ranch. There are no roads there. I have long suspected that there was another portal in that area but was never able to devote enough time to the search. Much evidence points to the probability of something there that is a generation point or portal of some kind.

The ranch then was ninety acres and was and is in the middle of many square miles of national forest land. The ranch sits in a secluded valley and most of the surrounding semi-arid desert is flat with areas of rolling hills. The Bradshaw Ranch is and was a one of a kind jewel among western ranches.

Vegetation in the area consists primarily of pinion pines, juniper trees, Arizona cypress, cottonwood trees, mesquite trees, prickly pear cactus, agave cactus, catsclaw bushes, sagebrush, tumbleweed and manzanita bushes—among many other shrubs and bushes.

I had parked my van on Bradshaw Hill above the ranch, and within minutes of off-the-road walking came upon the tire tracks of an all terrain vehicle—an ATV. It was one of those four tired, four wheel drive models. I didn't think anything of it because ATV's are as common as rattlesnakes around here.

I kept following the tracks since they were going in the same direction that I was. A little further on, I came upon a fifty foot length of olive drab half-inch nylon rope. It must have fallen off the ATV. Near the rope, I found on the ground an odd metallic piece of something the likes of which I have never seen before. It was about the size of a quarter and was gold and silver. It looked electronic.

The further I went, my interest became more heightened because the ATV tracks were headed exactly where I had planned to go. Then I came on to a third mystery that began to make me a little edgy.

I found a Z-shaped trench dug eight inches deep into a moderately sloping hillside. This was rock-hard ground, so somebody went to a lot of trouble to dig it. It was the same sort of thing someone would dig around a tent for drainage in case it rained. But a tent would hardly fit into that Z and the hillside was far too steep and rocky to sleep on. It was a long roll in a sleeping bag to the bottom of that hill.

I looked out over the desert and where I stood one could see about three hundred degrees. It was a good panorama of the surrounding lower desert from there. And the spot where I stood could be seen for miles from the east, south and west. And, it was overlooking precisely the area of the region's strangest paranormal activity. Odd—to say the least. But why? Why did someone dig that Z right there? It made no sense.

Preferring to go in a different direction at that point, I turned and walked to the west. I was going to make a wide circle around the south end of the ranch and come back to about where I was then.

I strolled about for an hour or so, then, looking at the sun, I realized I only had about ninety minutes of daylight left. Soon, I again came upon the ATV tracks. The tracks continued on down a dry wash and then out into the open desert. A one way trip. They must have had a second vehicle waiting to pick them up somewhere to the south.

Shadows were growing longer as the sun was now sinking lower on the horizon. And, it was one of the few times I had a gun with me. Not sure why I brought it but I did. It was my 30 caliber M-1 carbine. It was standard military issue in World War II, Korea and Vietnam. I bought it new right after I got out of high school. It felt good in my hand right then because something was feeling increasingly odd that afternoon. I hadn't told anyone where I was going and I was a long way from the road.

A bit of paranoia was growing in my brain as I made

haste to get back to my van. I was walking along at a fast pace not really paying attention to much, when I realized I was looking at something on the ground that was extremely out of the ordinary. I stopped, and with a glance took in the entire area around me. I was standing in a deep and wide, sandy bottomed arroyo that had been swept by countless floods over the centuries.

Footprints surrounded me in the fine white/gray sand. I saw that many of them were barefoot tracks sunk deep into the ground. I bent down to look closer at the tracks and an icy chill filled my chest. Paranoia shifted into high gear. I was looking at a bipedal footprint that was not in any way human. I have good photos of them.

Each track was twelve inches long, V-shaped and had five perfectly round toes, each about the size of a large grape. I put my hiking boot next to one track and put my full weight on that foot. My two hundred pound weight barely left an impression on the hard packed dry sand. But the barefoot tracks sunk in one to two inches. I estimated the weight of the owner of the track to be about eight hundred pounds. Eight hundred pounds on a twelve inch foot? I believe that is anatomically impossible for our Earth life zone. It seemed to me then that the owner of the track was native to another dimension, place, or planet, where density was much less important than on our Earth. These particular tracks have not only been seen by myself but by at least a half dozen other people in the Sedona area over the past two years. Including two expert wilderness guides.

These tracks that I was looking at may have been weeks old, days old,—or hours old! There are times when I'm not enthusiastic about being alone and that time was one of them. It seemed like there were hidden faces in the trees and bushes everywhere I looked. Runaway paranoia. Am I being dramatic? You bet! You should have been there!

I counted each of the barefoot tracks, there were forty-six. I scrutinized my immediate surroundings closely. I found where the two legged being had left the area. It had walked up a steep, sandy hillside. Only the first four or five inches of the front of the foot was deeply impressed into the sand. The hillside was saturated with water in several places and the ball of each foot and the five toes were perfectly preserved in form.

My curiosity not satiated, I went back to where the tracks were clustered the thickest. There seemed to me to be two men who wore size eleven running shoes. The company name was in the center of each footprint there in the fine sand. I felt there were two men because one set of tracks looked different, different weight maybe. And there seemed to be more tracks than one person would normally make.

As I stood there tying to comprehend this latest strangeness, a sudden realization struck me like a thunderbolt. Did the running shoes get there first—or did the creature—or did they all meet there at the same time?! That possibility tripled my paranoia. And—were they still close by and what sort of exotic weapons or cameras might be aimed at me that very moment.

I looked at the camera that was in my one hand and the military rifle in the other. No ordinary hiker! I could be seen for a hundred yards or more in several directions. That was enough for me. I made a hasty retreat back to my van and wasted no time getting back to town. On the way I glanced in my rear view mirror dozens of times. I hadn't forgotten that local researcher Rob Meyer had photographed an olive drab Humvee, with two men standing in back of it dressed in camouflage outfits, just a few weeks before. That photo had been taken less than a quarter mile from where I had parked my van that day.

As I write this, I am quite amazed at how many bipedal creature accounts/incidents that have actually occurred in the general area where I was between Red Canyon and Casner Mountain. And, for some unknown reason these creatures don't seem to get along with horses very well. At least not in this area. I have not heard of this exact same sort of activity happening anywhere else.

Several years ago Chris O'Brien of Crestone, Colorado and I were at his house comparing mental notes of horse, cattle and two legged creature incidents that we knew of. Chris has written several books on paranormal activity in the San Luis Valley in southeast Colorado. There seems to be a great similarity in paranormal activity in the San Luis Valley and in Sedona. Except that in the San Luis Valley there have been many bizarre cattle mutilations and virtually none (confirmed) in the Sedona area.

Chris had recently investigated an incident where a workhorse was found dead wedged into a V shaped tree. It had starved to death. It seemed to Chris and I that something certainly must have been chasing the horse. Work horses are huge, gentle animals and this one had been particularly known for its gentleness.

We have had a few of those types of horse/creature incidents in the Sedona area, some of which I have written about in depth. Right after *Merging Dimensions* was published there were several more of these *Twilight Zone* horse related episodes in this area.

Such as these. In the winter of 1996 Linda Bradshaw drove out to feed their horses and found one of them, a brown mare, wedged under a low lying limb in a juniper tree. Linda and Bob tried to coax and pull the horse out from under the limb, but in the end they had to saw off the eight inch limb so that the horse could get free. It was stuck that tight. It seemed to Linda and I that something big had chased the horse. We looked for unusual tracks but the free roaming horses had trampled the ground in that area thoroughly.

On the Bradshaw Ranch their horses were often allowed to run loose so they could roam freely around the fenced ranch. Linda and I on a number of occasions, while we were out doing our night photo flashing, would hear some or all of the horses running at full speed out in the desert. With prickly pear cactus, agave, Spanish bayonet and catsclaw all over the place, a horse knows that running fast at night in a desert is an enormously risky business.

One pitch black, moonless night (I remember well) four or five horses running at full speed passed within twenty feet of Linda and I. "Something" had to have been chasing them—they were running as if being chased. They were not out simply having a fun run.

And—until I saw the following myself I had had a hard time believing the stories. Something was literally ripping or biting off the manes of local ranch horses. It looked as if a handful of mane was grabbed and torn off leaving the remaining mane three or four inches long. I closely inspected several local ranch horses and it was exactly as I had just described. What on earth can catch and/or hold a thousand pound horse and bite, tear, or cut its mane off?! Other than the torn manes the horses were not physically harmed.

Looking for a simple reason, I asked concerned area ranchers who had been around horses all their lives. Not one could offer a logical explanation for the torn off manes. During my investigations, I found that in many of the cases all of the mane was torn off all the way from the horses ears down to its shoulders.

More Bigfoot Type Stories

On the Bradshaw Ranch is an old western town movie set/location where segments of many 1950's and 1960's western movies were shot. Actresses and actors such as Elvis Presley, Henry Fonda, Randolph Scott, Rock Hudson, Robert Mitchum, Cornel Wilde, John Wayne, Rhonda Fleming, Joan Crawford, Yvonne DeCarlo, Maureen O'Hara, Jimmy Stewart, Lee Marvin, Robert DeNiro and Sterling Hayden starred in, or acted in movies that were shot on or near the Bradshaw Ranch. There were actually many more actors and actresses than I have listed here. In total over fifty full length motion pictures were shot in the area. Bob Bradshaw himself worked as a cowboy actor in many of these movies. Sometimes as a double for the lead actor—the star of the movie.

One day Linda and I had gone out to the old western town for some reason I don't recall. Our specific destination was the old saloon. Linda had often told me about her interactions with a friendly white Bigfoot that Linda had given the name, Big Girl. Up to that point, to be honest, as much as I trusted and respected Linda, I had a real hard time with the whole Big Girl scenario.

Linda had gotten only fleeting glimpses of the white creature who to this day I'm not convinced was actually a Bigfoot. I think (hunch) it was some sort of other, perhaps related, huge bipedal creature.

Linda had told me, and shown me, how Big Girl would often leave her (Linda) long sticks arranged in geometric patterns. Big Girl would also at times leave her body prints in soft sand (see photo in *Merging Dimensions*). Linda explained to me how Big Girl would often rap on a tree trunk or a fence post with a heavy stick three times to get Linda's attention. It was also a greeting of sorts. It was always three raps. Linda would leave food for the Bigfoot such as grapes, lettuce and celery. Then in the morning where the food had been was the geometric pattern of sticks that was not there the day before.

It's pretty hard for simple desert creatures like jackrabbits, mice, deer, skunks or javelina to arrange sticks in consistent geometrical patterns.

So Linda and I were walking away from the town. I must emphasize that there were absolutely no other humans nearby—when three booming raps came from the center of the old town. And I mean booming. It sounded like someone, very strong, had picked up a six foot two-by-four and had hit the side of a wooden building with it as hard as they could. It was a dead calm sunny hot day. There was no wind blowing that day, not a breeze.

After that I was a complete believer. I never doubted or questioned anything Linda told me after that day.

Bigfeet Hate Guns

This is sort of a rather amusing story I had almost forgotten. At the onset of the mysterious paranormal events at the Bradshaw Ranch, some of the ranch hands thought that many of the things that Linda and I were experiencing, photographing, and talking about were a complete crock of B.S.

Especially the stories of Big Girl, the White Bigfoot.

So one day during deer hunting season some of the boys decided to go deer hunting on the ranch. Bigfeet hate guns. Linda told me that once.

The boys left from the ranch house and were gone fifteen minutes, when a siren like (Bigfoot) scream arose that could be heard from the direction that the boys had gone in. Linda told how the scream could even be clearly heard inside the ranch house. She said just minutes later the boys were back at the ranch house and were as white as ghosts. She said they put their high powered rifles in the corner of the room and as they left for town they exclaimed, "OK. WE BELIEVE! WE BELIEVE!"

This is a good time to bring up skeptics again. It's one of my favorite subjects. Narrow minded people. Until some people witness first hand some of the things I have been describing, they will never—and I mean never—believe. Over the years there have been dozens and dozens of people who I have known deeply, or casually, and who were fundamentalist skeptics until they had a personal, direct, paranormal experience. Such as the ones I've had.

Then they joined what I call "The Family." You can go anywhere on this Earth and meet someone for the very first time, and because they have had experiences similar to yours, it is instantly like you have known each other all of your lives.

You know each other, like a beloved brother or sister.

There are no formalities, no awkwardness, you both feel comfortable and right at home with each other. Family. I have experienced this sort of thing countless times now. There is often even a deep feeling of affection.

I would have greatly enjoyed to have engraved-in-stone skeptics like Phil Klass or Carl Sagan standing beside me when some of the things I have been talking about were going on right in front of us. I would have said—with gusto— "Well ... what do you think of that?!!!" I'm sure the reply would have been educational.

I have given a number of lectures. I seldom do it anymore. It's just not something I like to do. Typically an audience reacts to me like this; half of them by the expressions on their faces think I am a totally whacked out fruitcake, and the other half are utterly fascinated, and think I am some sort of hero, guru, or something.

I have grown very tired of the... this-guy-is-nuts-let-him-prove-it-to-me non-believers. I guess I just really don't give a rat's ass anymore. Let 'em find out on their own now.

I did a talk once to an audience of two hundred who

were mostly UFO researchers. I got the same "let's burn him at the stake/hero" reactions. That night at dinner in an enormous dining hall, a guy who was talking to some people at a table in the middle of the room raised his voice so that everybody in the place could hear him. He was still looking at the people he was talking to when he said, "YEAH! WE OUGHT TO TAKE THE BASTARD OUT AND SHOOT HIM!" Everybody in the place knew who he was talking about.

Cowboy/Red Ferrari Story

Sort of in conjunction with the previous, in 1992 I had a strange encounter and it wasn't with a space alien. A rumor had gotten out and had traveled far and wide that I was in possession of a video—shot near Sedona—that showed strange, deep space aliens walking around in the desert with a good shot of their parked spacecraft in the background

I did indeed have an extraordinary UFO related video which eventually got me on national TV, but it wasn't at all what the rumors were portraying. I had a real good time with this because I had heard some of the fermented rumors when they came back around. I simply smiled slyly when asked. Just for the sheer hell of it I wanted to see how far the whole thing would go. I wasn't worried, it wasn't going to damage my excellent credibility any. Few people asked if I really had a video like that—they just wanted to see it.

I got a phone message one day at my answering service. I had been tipped off earlier so I knew what to expect. A man had heard—through the grapevine—about the video I had and urgently wanted to talk to me about it. He wanted to buy me dinner and drinks at Enchantment Resort in Boynton Canyon, one of the most exclusive joints in Sedona. Not being one to pass up a free meal and what was sure to be an interesting experience, I agreed to meet the man.

I got there on time and the tall, thin, white haired man was patiently waiting for me at a table. When he stood up he sort of resembled Abe Lincoln. I could tell by the way that the staff was fawning over him that he was a very important ($$$) man. He was. He was an international media mogul. Big time. He was dressed like an 1880's hard rock miner or placer gold prospector. I thought that maybe his mule was tied up in the back somewhere.

His whole outfit was worn, just like a miner, right down to his sombrero like Montana cut cowboy hat, faded grey vest, red neckerchief, now pink red shirt and big shiny worn belt buckle. His high mileage blue jeans were tucked into knee high cowboy boots that were almost worn through at the heels. The leather was worn white around the heels. I thought he was probably a Fifth Avenue executive from New York City.

To my surprise he turned out to be a native Arizonan. His brand new red Ferrari was cooling off out in the parking lot. I'm sure I had an interesting look on my face.

After a pleasant meal and a lot of drinks (this guy could drink like a dehydrated sponge) he finally got to the point I had been expecting.

He revealed that he knew about the video I had and he felt it was my duty to give it to him, "to get the word out, people need to know!" This guy had enough money to buy just about anything he wanted. But he never offered me ten cents for rights to the "Video". At the time I was so broke I was living in my van out in the desert, and I knew that he knew it. I guess he figured I would leap at anything that was tossed my way. He made me a polished sales pitch that made it sound like the chance of a lifetime, and for him it would have been.

What did sound like fun was that he was going to rent two helicopters and film (interview) me from one while I pointed excitedly to the spot where I had videotaped the aliens and their spaceship. But no money was ever mentioned. It would have taken up two or three days of my time. If I did indeed possess such a video it would have meant untold millions for him and his media network. Several times I thought to myself, "I wonder if he really thinks I'm that stupid?"

So anyway, he and I ate and drank plenty, ran up a god-awful tab, and after a while I could tell by his demeanor, that he concluded that it was a hopeless cause, trying to make me see the light.

After a while we forgot the whole thing and drifted into a different realm of discussion. We both ended up having a very good time. All in all he turned out to be a damn nice guy—after he dropped the corporate bull shit.

Another Strange Creature Episode

I just tell 'em like they happened. I'm not sensationalizing any of these stories. Some are weird enough and hard enough to believe as they are. This next one would stretch anyone's sensibilities.

In the old western town was a small gift shop in a fifteen by fifteen-foot building. It was filled with the usual tourist type trappings of nuts, candy, gum, postcards, and other knick-knacks. At the time all of that stuff had been in there for a year or more and was pretty stale. At that time the old town had been closed to tourists for quite a while. At the time of this writing (Feb. 2000), the old town, and the ranch, is again open to tourists and is being run by Bob Bradshaw's sons. It is called, "A Day in the West". Tourists are picked up in Sedona and are driven out to the site. There are negotiations, at the moment, by the City of Sedona (and others) to purchase the Bradshaw Ranch. In the years ahead it is anybody's guess what will be out there.

What led into this next episode, Linda called me one day and exclaimed the words I so often heard, and was always thrilled to the depths of my soul to hear. In an excited tone she would always begin with, "Tom! You are not going to believe this!!" Those words quickly turned many potentially boring and depressing days into exciting ones for me.

As always, I jumped into my van with camera, flash lights, batteries, recording equipment and a dozen other items I always kept in a backpack. This set-up could be grabbed and thrown into my van at a moment's notice.

I got out to the ranch and Linda was waiting for me at the front door. I knew it was going to be good. She said what she wanted to show me was at the western town. I shouldered my backpack that contained my research equipment and we walked to the old western town. It's about a fifteen minute walk from the ranch house.

As we walked, Linda patiently, as always, explained to me what she had found. She had removed the padlock from the front door of the gift shop and had gone in. She told me the place looked as if it had been burglarized. The floor was littered with gift shop items that had previously been on shelves and were now scattered all over the floor. Few things had been left untouched or unbroken.

What had immediately struck her as odd was that only three people knew where the padlock key was, herself, Bob and her son, Victor. The building showed no signs of breaking and entering. No windows were broken and the front and back doors were undamaged and were securely locked.

Linda and I got to the gift shop and went in. It was just as she had described it. Then she pointed out what I had already surmised. If she, or Bob, or Victor, or anyone else in the family had wanted any of that stuff, all they had to do was open the door and go in and get what they wanted. The whole otherworldly scenario began to take shape in my mind at about the same time Linda remarked, "Whoever, or whatever, got in here did it without breaking in." In simpler terms "it" probably walked right through the door or walls. Like a ghost.

Of all the bizarre paranormal events I have ever personally investigated this was in a category all its own. I have never heard of, or read of, any other incident like this one. As I pawed through the rubble on the floor the whole thing got weirder and weirder. Whatever had gotten in there had, in a space of two or three days, eaten hundreds of those red jawbreaker, hard candy fireballs that have a peppery taste on the outside and are peppery sweet in the center. They are about the size of a quarter in diameter. Not only that, but "it" had also eaten hundreds of those colored penny bubble gum balls we used to buy in the round glass dispensers.

So I'm standing there thinking if it had walked through the walls—like a ghost—how in blazes did it walk back through the wall with ten plus pounds of bubble gum and pepper balls in its stomach?

Some packrats and mice had indeed gotten in there. They no doubt smelled the spilled candy. A small hole was chewed through at the base of one wall. A few wrappers showed unmistakable signs of being chewed on by little teeth. But whatever had perpetrated the crime had un-screwed ten inch wide lids on the gift shop's gallon size plas-tic containers to get at the contents inside. Packrats and mice can't do that. "It" had apparently dumped out the con-tents of each jar and sat there on the floor with these piles of pepper balls around it, then simply squeezed one end of each clear cellophane wrapper and popped the jawbreakers into its mouth. Ninety percent of the wrappers had been blown out at one end. I don't think rats can do that.

Had a human, any human, sat there and consumed that much stale candy and stale bubble gum in a few days, they would have to be crazy for one thing and would probably be dead on the floor from a sugar and rubber rush for another. I saved a quart freezer bag full of those wrappers. I look at them once in a while as proof to myself that it actually hap-pened. Plus, Linda and I shot two rolls of film of the interior of the gift shop before we disturbed anything.

Had it been just this one event one could simply rationalize it all somehow—and forget it. But when taken in context with all the other strange, unexplainable things that happened on the ranch, the gift shop event takes on an even stranger note.

They Were Watching Us

This next event is another which has a category all of its own in a long saga of ultra bizarre occurrences. Linda and I had remarked to each other on many occasions after witnessing paranormal phenomena that if we hadn't had each other as a witness—we would have thought we were losing our minds. And this entire case certainly doesn't involve just Linda and I either. There had been in those two years dozens of people who at times shared with us as eye witnesses to this parade of supernormal events. Including one spellbound Fox network camera crew.

It was another one of those warm, still, and fragrant summer nights full with the spicy and earthy sweet smells of the high desert. Linda and I were standing out in the front yard of the ranch house taking random flash shots while we talked. There was a pause in the conversation, and a sudden thought came to me (I have often wondered where sudden thoughts really originate from).

It came to me that with all the thousands of flash photos we had taken with the cameras, and all the probings we had done with our 1.5 million candlepower spotlights, we had never shined the spotlights straight up! For a few moments I pondered this great revelation with a measure of anticipation and excitement. What if, I thought, we shined these lights straight up—lights that were more powerful than an automobile's headlights on high beam—and they revealed the bottom of a huge space craft silently sitting directly above our heads.

In my mind I fantasized all sorts of boundless possibilities. Hardly able to restrain my excitement I blurted out, "Linda! You know what? We have never shined these lights straight up into the sky!" There was a pause and I could see that Linda was thinking exactly the same thoughts as I was. She shortly replied, "You know, you're right. Let's do it!"

So in unison we turned on the spotlights and shined them vertically into the night sky. We both got an instant jolt of absolute bewilderment at what we saw. It was not, at all, what we had expected. And of all the wondrous and unconventional things we had witnessed out in the desert, what we saw right then our minds could not comprehend.

About five feet above us were four silvery capsule like objects each about an inch and a half long. They were slowly circling over our heads in a strange liquid-like movement. We recognized instantly that the way these things moved they could not possibly be insects of any kind. These things were shaped exactly like a large vitamin capsule one would buy in a store, but were four or five times larger. They were a dull mercury-like color. We both experienced and expressed utter confusion as we watched these things circling above us.

Five seconds after our lights had hit the silvery capsules, they began to quickly disperse. Two flew away at such speed that they were gone in an eye blink. The third began to rise up higher and we followed along with the spotlights as it shot over the top of a thirty foot tall juniper tree to our right. The fourth object moved far slower and it actually descended down to about eight feet off the ground. I walked along with it, my spotlight not twenty inches underneath it. In fact, I got so close to it that at one point I very easily could have jumped up and grabbed it.

As I walked along under it I battled in my mind whether to try to reach up and grab the object. But hesitation and fear set in. I was thinking I might get badly burned—or electrocuted—or something. Anything that strange might have a built in defense system. Especially if it was of alien origin. Everytime I think of that event I wonder if I should have grabbed the thing and what might have happened. What a piece of evidence it might have been! Was that the reason it went so slow, it wanted me to have it? Or, was it baiting me on so I would have ended up like a piece of bacon? Or worse.

Caution is perhaps always the best way, but Linda and I never saw those silver capsules (or for that matter anything like that again) when we shined our spotlights straight up.

We had caught the strange capsules off guard. How many nights had they been up there.... and what else besides silver capsules had perhaps been unknowingly hovering over our heads?

Linda and I

It is appropriate in this book to include something about the working relationship that Linda Bradshaw and I had. Contrary to juicy rumors navigating amongst imaginative soap opera minds in town, Linda and I never had a romantic relationship in any form. But the relationship we did have was quite extraordinary.

Men and women have deep and basic differences which are awkward under the very best of circumstances. But Linda and I were so compatible, and alike, we very often had the exact same emotions and thoughts at the same time, even if we were many miles separated. Some of these thoughts and emotions were intense. Personally, I have had all my life rather intense thoughts and feelings anyway and I suffer from periods of extreme depression. And so does Linda. There were days that I would call her on random matters and it would almost always turn out that she was thinking and feeling at the same time, precisely, what I was. We were so alike in every aspect that we would often joke that we must have come from the same planet. And maybe we have. Linda is a person of great compassion, gentility, intelligence, integrity and fairness. Man or woman, these days, those are fine qualities. She was a terrific partner through all this.

A Meeting With A UFO

This next UFO incident is probably the most poignant and personal that I have yet experienced. And perhaps the most dramatic as well. I have now seen well over fifty different flying objects and lights that were of alien strangeness. I have seen six UFO's that I am certain were alien crafts. These six were actual, physical ships of different sizes and colors. All were disc-shaped.

One early fall evening in 1996 I had been down to the ranch visiting and had shot a few rolls of film while I was there. I usually made a point of leaving for home by 9:30 p.m. or 10:00 p.m. so that I could get a decent night's sleep. Late at night it was a long, dark, dusty drive back to town. But this particular night had passed quickly and it was after midnight by the time I left the ranch. The dirt road out of the ranch to the "main road" (the main road is another dirt road often as rough, or worse, than the ranch road, particularly after heavy rain) is a distance of nearly a mile and it was slow going. I usually drove about ten m.p.h. The road winds out of the hidden valley where the ranch sits, goes up to the top of Bradshaw Hill and then down a quarter mile to the main dirt road which is Loy Butte Road.

I would always stop at the top of Bradshaw Hill to take a pee or just get out to admire the view. Day or night it is one of the most spectacular desert panoramas on this planet. A number of automobile commercials have been shot on top of that hill. Not long ago this country's best selling luxury car company filmed a commercial on top of Bradshaw Hill. They built a twenty- foot tower to put their cameras on in order to get different angles for their shots. They evidently didn't care for the red dirt look so they covered the whole top of the hill with green astroturf so that the luxury car looked like it was parked on a lawn in New York—or somewhere.

As I was standing on top of the hill preparing to go, I noticed a peculiar light on the eastern horizon. As tired as I was by then, I kept watching the light. I think by now I have seen just about everything there is to see in the night sky, and when something is really odd it catches my eye immediately. This light would come towards me and then retreat back to the horizon, a back and forth distance of forty miles or more. This went on for a half hour. The light came forward and then pulled back at least ten times. This strange behavior bothered me because it was something I had never seen before. Finally, I said to hell with it all and headed for home.

I had driven a mile and made the turn from Loy Butte Road on to Boynton Pass Road. I went another quarter mile and to my consternation there was the light again. This time it was close. It appeared to be less than a mile away.

And it was exactly pacing the speed of my van. As I drove along this was starting to bother me a great deal. If you have read the alien abduction books this light-through-the-trees-following-your-car scenario is the classic lead-in to an abduction. I wondered to myself what I should do? Go back to the ranch? Linda and Bob had gone to bed by then and I really needed to get back to town. I had a busy day coming up.

So as I drove on, I worked up a glowing anger. I said to myself, why does this stuff always have to happen in the middle of the night on a road out in the middle of nowhere? Why can't they, whoever "they" are, do this crap in broad daylight? I was becoming highly irritated—pissed off. I felt like a sitting duck, and I was dead tired, hungry, and now in a very bad mood. When I am dead tired and hungry, God Himself could appear before me and I wouldn't care a whit. When my energy is gone—it's gone.

I drove on and lost sight of the UFO. It seemed to have left. Good! I was relieved. I could just forget the whole thing now and go on home and go to bed.

I was coming up on Doe Mesa, and my thoughts had shifted to more mundane matters of the next day's business. I came around a corner out of a deep dip in the road and into the wide open area of desert below Doe Mesa.

And there it was!!

At the sight of it I had a few seconds of ice cold fear. Now it was not simply a light in the far distance, but an ominous disc-shaped craft about fifty feet in diameter. It had a series of red, white and orange lights flashing or steadily glowing along its top, bottom and outer perimeter.

The ship was now so low that it was actually lower than the top of Doe Mesa. Which was about a hundred vertical feet higher than where I was. The ship was flying at an extremely slow speed. It didn't take me long to figure out that the craft was on an intercept course with me. In about three hundred yards our paths would cross on Boynton Pass Road. Then what?! I wondered. As I drove very slowly along I stared intently at the craft. All sorts of mixed thoughts and feelings were going through my mind. In a flash of anger borne out of tiredness, I said in my mind, "I am just not in a mood for this kind of shit tonight!"

At the exact instant I finished those words in my mind, the craft stopped dead in the air. Then seconds later it reversed its course. In less than five seconds it disappeared behind some low hills ten miles to the east. For a few moments I was electrified with the realization that they had heard my thoughts! They were no doubt listening to my thoughts all along. And "they" had respected my wish.

I stopped the van in the middle of the road and got out. I dumbly stared at the spot in the distance where the craft had disappeared. However, to this day I do not regret my actions of that night. If they wanted to interact with me they could not have picked a worse time. Whoever they were their judgement was off. It's called courtesy and common sense. Maybe where they came from their etiquette and procedures are different from ours. If they had given me some advance warning, or some slight sort of notice, everything would have been different. I never saw that craft again. Did I miss the opportunity of a lifetime or lifetimes? Maybe. But I still don't regret it.

If "they" want to interact with me let it be in broad daylight when my mind is clear and I feel up to speed. I would dearly love to have a positive interaction with aliens, but not at 1 a.m., 2 a.m., 3 a.m., or 5 a.m. I have never seen a physical alien (that I consciously remember) but I have come so close on many occasions. They have always stayed just one step ahead of me.

There are plenty of aliens among us. This book—these words will go all around the world. So I say to aliens of a positive and compassionate nature, let's talk anytime. In the daytime. Anywhere you choose.

Another Missed Meeting?

This next encounter is similar to the last one in that it started out on Bradshaw Hill. But this incident evaporated very quickly.

Several months after the Doe Mesa/UFO encounter, I was driving up to Bradshaw Hill about the same time of night. It was about midnight. I looked down to Loy Butte Road, and a half mile further down the road two enormous balls of white light were hovering stationary over the road-way. One light was no more than fifty feet above the road. The second light was off at a slight angle and was a hundred feet higher than the other. They seemed to be just sitting out there waiting for me. They looked ominous.

I sat in my van in the dark with the motor off staring at those two lights through my windshield. Normally I had shot all of my film down on the ranch and that night was no different. I was out of film again. Like the time before, I said to myself, screw it—I'm going to go for it. I drove halfway toward the lights. I looked away once and when I looked back, they were gone. Or they had just turned the light off and were sitting up there in the dark. I drove all the way home with no further incidents.

CHAPTER SIX

The Incredible Sedona Lights

I've lived in Sedona now for over thirteen years. The stories of flying or stationary balls of light of many sizes and colors have been so numerous over the years, it was difficult to select the incidents I will include here. These incidents and sightings have been in the thousands. The ones I will write about here are ones I have first hand knowledge of and was personally involved with. And remember, it's not just words. I have an enormous collection of photos to back up what I say. In the world of paranormal research, this is exceedingly rare. Not to mention hundreds of eye witness accounts.

There was one strange, eerie and beautiful light I was never able to get a photograph of. Many people tried to get a photo of this light, but as far as I know no one ever succeeded. This light seemed to know people were trying to get a shot of it. It would always blink out just before the shutter was tripped or the camcorder was focused. This light was always seen in the same section of desert roughly two miles southwest of Bradshaw Hill.

It was a stunning, shimmering display of fireworks light that had all the colors of the rainbow in it. This was a sphere of round light that was about ten feet in diameter. It would appear abruptly and sit out there in the desert about a hundred feet off the ground. Whatever it was it was breathtakingly beautiful. It hasn't been seen since 1996 and whether it will reappear again someday is anyone's guess.

The Elusive Red Fire Light

In the early spring of 1997 there were many stories of campers or UFO buffs seeing a strange red light flying around, or sitting stationary out in the desert between Red Canyon and Casner Mountain. I began to take special notice of these accounts when fellow researcher Chris Montez and her husband had this light fly to within yards of them. They were camped near Red Canyon, when one of these red lights came out of nowhere and flew straight towards them. Chris said the light acted as if it was curious about what they were doing. It seemed to be checking them out. It sat out there in the air for awhile, made a U-turn and then flew away. This light was about two feet in diameter. According to Chris the sight of it shocked her husband right down to his shoes. It always does the first time you see one of these things.

About that same time, my former girlfriend and her son had gone out to that very spot camping. They wanted to see if they could get a glimpse of the light that so many people were talking about. And, with a basic point and shoot camera she took a once in a lifetime, awesome, photo of the red ball of light. Incredibly, the sphere appeared directly behind and above a large juniper tree just yards from where they were camped. She didn't think it was much of a big deal.

She took the shot right through the branches of the tree and the light was no more than a hundred yards away. I groaned when I saw the photo because with the telephoto lens and low light camera and film I have I could have gotten at least six stunning photos of the light. I had by then spent five nights out in that area looking for the light and saw nothing. Zip! Zero!! And on the very first night she gets a mind blowing shot with 400 speed film and a point and shoot camera. The flash had even gone off lighting up the tree.

Ultimately, I spent fourteen nights out in the desert before I finally encountered the elusive red light. The first time I saw it was simply too far away to get a good photo of it. But that light, after hearing about it and seeing it once, was like no other light I have ever seen. It looked like a spherical bonfire in the sky. But it had more brilliant reds and yellows than a camp type wood fire. Finally on June 14, 1997, I got a satisfactory photo of the light. About

10:00 p.m. it appeared over the dome rock called Robber's Roost (it is called Robber's Roost because there was a shoot-out there between outlaws and a sheriff's posse in the late 1800's). Robber's Roost is directly below Casner Mountain, ten miles southwest of Sedona.

The red light was over two miles away. I shot six photos of it with 1000 speed film. I used a 500 mm telephoto lens and used a five second exposure on each shot. Only one shot came out good but it is spectacular. I wanted to include the photo in this book but a red light against a dark gray/green/black background will not reproduce in black and white.

I had originally planned to do a separate book called *The Incredible Sedona Lights*. I was going to go into a review and introspection on the several well written books and other published theories that these lights are simply natural, Earth aerial lights (ball lightning for example) or are created by the friction of deep lying earthquake faults. I will agree that no doubt a small percentage of these lights are created by some localized, natural activity. However, from my own personal experience (and Linda Bradshaw's), I can say without any doubt or hesitation, that these lights are for the most part a life form we know absolutely nothing about. Most of them are some type of living creature. Period. I have been as close to these lights as any person on this planet. Many of these lights display high interactive intelligence and even at times a liberal sense of humor.

In 1997 I spent six solid months, at night, playing cat and mouse with glowing white spheres of light. These lights would blink on high in the air, or rise up out of the trees in the Nolan Tank area of the desert southwest of Sedona (a tank, in cattle ranch terms, is a bulldozed saucer shaped hole in the ground that collects rainwater for cattle to drink). Some of these lights would fly around some, then either blink out or fly off into the distance. Clearly, after observing for so long, it was evident to me that most of these lights originated from the same point—or points. This would indicate some sort of entrance point, or portal.

What took so long to figure out was how far away, from me, these lights actually were. I could not tell if it was one mile or twenty miles. After many nights and hundreds of photographs (all 300mm or 500mm telephoto) I discovered that there were actually two distinct types of these off-white spheres. Some were indeed a mile or less away, and some were actually twenty or thirty miles away. It was hard to get close to these things because they seem to know when they are being watched. The most distant ones would rise up behind Mingus Mountain, which was ten air miles distant from me. These particular distant lights were enormous. They were probably twenty-five feet in diameter. The mile away lights, same off-white glowing color, were one foot to three feet in diameter.

One five minute night exposure photo I took in the summer of 1997 was of a cluster of five of the enormous white lights. During the five minutes the camera shutter was open these lights, moving in different directions, made for a spectacular photograph. This photo was ultimately seen by many millions of people worldwide. I had given it, free, during an interview for a network TV show. The photo, among others, went out to other syndicates, including BBC in Europe and on to Japanese TV.

After a while, I had decided to concentrate my efforts on the distant lights, as they seemed more interesting. More intriguing, I suppose. The very last night I spent chasing these lights was one of the most singularly preternatural nights of my life. One out of many.

It was in mid-October of 1997. I was determined to get as close to these big spheres of light as I possibly could. I especially wanted to discover where they originated from— with caution.

First Was a Phantom Jet

I had located, one day while driving around, an open field-like area halfway between Cottonwood and Camp Verde. The spot was just yards from the Verde River. Several nights later I went back and saw that I had a good clear angle at the five miles away Mingus Ridge. Just beyond that high ridge (6000 feet—I was at 3500 feet) was where the lights were coming from. I never did determine where the big spheres actually originated from, but a good guess would be somewhere in the vicinity of the tiny, and spooky (spook lights, ghost lights?) hamlet of Cherry. Cherry was once an important overland stage coach stop. Even in high times, past Cherry there was nothing but a narrow horse and buggy dirt road on the 130 miles from Flagstaff to Phoenix. The world and freeways have now bypassed Cherry. It remains on a secluded, narrow, and mountainous gravel road. All in all, a bit of a strange place. A proper place for stygian spheres of light to rise out from.

It was dusk when I got to the open area I had located near the Verde River. I got my tripod, camera and 500mm lens set up and waited for whatever might appear over Mingus Ridge. About an hour after dark, a thin layer of ground fog began to develop in the surrounding area. Unusual ground fogs always make me real nervous. In some of the most malevolent paranormal activity around the world, ghost-like fogs were often present at the same time. Ground fogs around here are never common. My nervousness was justified—things got stranger.

The fog got fairly dense but not enough to make me leave. I could still shoot through it with the camera. About 8:00 p.m. I heard a sizeable jet aircraft coming in my direction. I waited, and in a few minutes I could see it approaching four to five thousand feet above me. It was a small two engine jet. It didn't seem to be a corporate jet, but more the type the military might use, the engines were out on the wings. Something else caught my eye and it gave me quite a start. About halfway between me and the small two engine jet was an airliner sized jet flying at the same speed of the smaller jet.

But the big jet made no sound whatsoever. It was like a phantom. It was not a reflection from the small jet because the larger jet's size and configuration was completely different. Looking up at all this through a layer of fog made it seem even more other-worldly. The bigger plane was flying at perhaps two thousand feet above the ground. Under normal circumstances this would be a difficult, if not impossible feat, because of the nearby Mingus Ridge and the chance of colliding with a light plane landing at the Cottonwood Airport. The smaller jet had flashing running lights on it—the lower airliner-sized jet had none at all.

During the time period between 1994 and 1997, phantom airliners and phantom jet fighters were seen a number of times around Sedona and the Verde Valley. Military exercises using hologram decoys perhaps?

In 1996 I was out on the Red Canyon Road about a mile off Highway 89-A. I was with two other people and the night was perfectly clear and there was a full moon. One of these phantom jets flew at low altitude right above us. It had two engines, one on each wing, it had standard strobe and running lights—but it made not the slightest sound. Was it a UFO imitating an aircraft? I believe that would be a good assumption as I have seen this sort of thing at least a dozen times widely spaced over the years.

Soon after the big and the small aircraft flew out of my sight, I turned and a sphere of light was rising above Mingus Ridge. I quickly busied myself taking still photos of it (I never did have a camcorder). To compound matters, several weeks before that particular night, I had the disturbing and discouraging discovery that some of these Mingus Ridge lights were actually commercial airliners taking off from Phoenix Sky Harbor Airport over a hundred miles away. But—it soon became all too evident that UFO's were mixing in with the airliners. This is nearly identical to the UFO/airplane activity over Pine Bush, New York. I have photos of some of these Mingus Ridge lights spiraling like a corkscrew miles into the night sky. Airliners don't fly in a tight corkscrew pattern.

The Phantom Spear

So I took a number of photos of lights rising from behind the ridge and things eventually quieted down. But not for long. About 11:00 p.m. I began thinking it was time to go home. I was scanning the surrounding flats with my binoculars, when I noticed something on the ground that was extremely not normal. It was a glowing object which then was barely visible. As the object brightened, what it looked like was an enormous spear that was jammed shaft end into the ground. The object was about eight feet in height and glowing brighter by the minute. Soon I could easily see it without binoculars. It was about a hundred yards away.

I went to my van and dug out my night vision binoculars. I switched them on, and waited until the high pitched whine of the capacitor stopped. Night vision devices turn dark night panoramas into eerie shades of soft greens. The spear-like object stood out like a lighthouse as I looked at it through the night vision binoculars. The thing grew brighter and brighter and caused me to look for a fast escape route. It looked like it was getting ready to do something. It gave me a creepy and strange sensation. I muttered out loud to myself, "If that fucking thing moves I'm out of here!" I was really fearful that it might start coming towards me. I took two photos of it. When I took the second shot, my Minolta SLR jammed—badly. I later had to take the camera to a photo repair shop to have the camera fixed. It had actually broken inside. I still have one of the photos of the object. It looks just like a warrior's spear stuck in the ground shaft end first. The glowing spear object didn't move. I left there and haven't been back. That particular night was the night I threw in the towel with the lights. After six months of chasing phantoms, enough was enough.

A factor that dawned on me recently (years later) was this...ancient Native Americans of the Verde Valley. These last few years I had connected the spear-like object with UFO's and the paranormal sky lights I had been chasing. Prehistoric Indians lived in that particular area beginning 10,000 years ago. Ancient tribes such as the Anasazi, Hohokam and Sinaqua have long since vanished from those grounds. Resident tribes are now the Apache and the Yavapai. In that same general area there have been some horrendous massacres. Some were by Indians against Indians, but most were by white settlers and the U.S. Army against Indians when the settlers arrived in the region in the late 1800's. So I have to wonder. Could that spear like object have been some sort of ancient Indian sign to me? And if it were, what was the meaning? I could ask a hundred different metaphysical people and local Indians around here and I would get a hundred and fifty different opinions. So I haven't asked.

Dr. Steven Greer

On the nights of November 30', December 1, and 2, 1998, Dr. Steven Greer M.D. and one of his CSETI (Center For The Study of Extraterrestrial Intelligence) teams were at the Bradshaw Ranch and at nearby Dry Creek. They were conducting exercises trying to establish contact with a UFO. Evidently at Dry Creek they did make contact with a white sphere. Flashing spotlight sequences were returned in like fashion by the white sphere. I have had to rely on accounts of those who were there, as I was not. Evidently that was the sole contact and not much came of it.

My "Ice Cube" Photo

In late October of 1997, Linda Bradshaw and I had one of our most dramatic experiences with these "playful" small white spheres. After we discovered that some of these enigmatic lights would respond to our spotlight Morse code type flashes, we got more and more creative. We even bought a plug-in strobe light, but found it to be totally ineffective other than irritating a few low flying light plane jocks.

There was one particular night that we were playing flash games with five of these skyborne lights. They were three or four hundred yards southeast of us and they were several hundred feet in the air. Five was not at all normal. We would usually get a response from one individual sphere at a time. Sometimes several would appear but usually only one would stay. If others did appear they would almost always vanish or fly away within minutes.

The five lights stayed around for quite a while. Over half an hour if I remember correctly. Normally, and this happened time after time, I would get a tripod adjusted and the camera focused, and the very instant I was going to snap the shutter—the light I was trying to photograph would either vanish (blink out) or jump out of the way. This sort of thing happened many times. However, this night the five lights stayed, came closer, and gradually spaced themselves out along the low ridge a few hundred yards to the south and stayed there—unmoving. They were spaced about two hundred feet apart.

The fifth light, the one closest to us, (to our pleasant surprise) began drifting closer towards Linda and I. To use a well-worn phrase, the sight was awesome. I could scarcely believe my luck. I had a full roll of high speed film in the camera and the camera was fitted with my 70—300mm zoom telephoto lens. The camera was on the tripod all ready to go. I carefully focused the lens on the blazing ball of light and made sure the exposure setting was correct.

This time the light did not jump away or vanish before I snapped the shutter. I took three photos of it. Good ones! Then all of the five lights along the ridge blinked out one by one. When the photo was developed, I expected a blazing light illuminating the surrounding area like a miniature sun. But instead, to my great surprise, what appeared on the photo was a glowing rectangular ice cube like object which looked as if it was back lit by many arc lights hidden behind the trees on the ridge.

What Is It!? I Don't Know!

The most common question I get asked when people look at one of my paranormal or other-worldly skyborne photos is, "What is it!!!" How the @#$ do I know what it is!? If I knew what it was I'd be rich and famous. Sometimes that question really frosts me. At times, out of sheer frustration I'll make something up like, "It's a Gazaktar phobo probe dispatched from an orbiting Boobian scout ship. The Boobian ship was piloted by dark agents from the sinister Chumptarian system." Then I'll stand there with a dead serious look on my face for a few moments—before I smile. Some of the replies and reactions would in themselves make a good book subject.

On a number of occasions someone has (unasked) taken copies of some of my photos to a channeler. Some of these channels were nationally known. And some of the responses still make me cringe. Gazaktars, Boobians and sinister dark Chumptarians pales in comparison with some of the incredible answers or definitions some of those people got. In eighty percent of the cases the channels channeled explanation was sheer, utter, absolute, total, complete, flaming bullshit. How do I know? Well, in some of the cases I did/do have a pretty good idea what the object in the photo was. Down the road some of these things in the photos proved to be something pretty mundane and easily explainable. But the channeled explanation of the object was that it was a flagship from the Zoomdah system containing the Goddess Zoomoverya herself, here on a mission to save the Earth, etc., etc. I won't go into the details of how often Linda and I were supposed to be going to get vaporized, or fall through cracks in time or dimensions if we kept up our photo work. It's too much for these pages. However, nothing bad ever happened to either Linda or myself. But, however, I have to say that I still believe in channeling. There are some channels in this country who are really channeling a wise, higher being. I am convinced of that.

However, ever since I discovered that my hero, the Tibetan Tuesday Lobsang Rampa never existed, I have to have substantial proof of anything important, particularly if it is anything of a spiritual or paranormal nature. It was more than a slight jolt to me when I discovered that Lobsang Rampa was a literary hoax. The hoax was perpetrated for many years by an Englishman named Cyril Henry Hoskin. Lobsang Rampa was Cyril Henry Hoskin. Hoskin was born in England in 1911 and died of heart trouble in Calgary, Alberta on January 25, 1981.

There are some of us who are going to great lengths to find the truth about who we really are, why we are here and who is it that is living amongst us that we cannot see. Then there are those who intentionally, knowingly, and jovially fabricate elaborate and heartbreaking hoaxes. What is worse in the long run—physical murder, or the kind of murder that subdues our spirit and souls? Hoaxes help to keep us in a stagnant state of uncertainty and distrust. Then where do we turn?

Many people go through life with beliefs based on hope, faith and trust. All well and good for some. Some people have channels telling them what is or what isn't. Some people have their shaman, spirit guides or angels or whatever telling them what is and what isn't. Some have psychics who dictate their lives. But I am one who must have proof, some sort of tangible proof.

I want to know as much as I can now that's provable. I don't want to get to the end of my life and then discover that most or all of my beliefs were completely erroneous or wrong.

I think we are being pulled into the future now, not pushed anymore. Pulled into the future by our collective past experiences whether negative or positive. We will soon see where the trail leads. Time may or may not be short, but we need answers to these questions I pose.

As I write about these extraordinary events I depict throughout this book, I am again struck with how common place and almost blase' these various incidents and sightings became—for myself and a number of others. For instance, one summer afternoon I was hiking with a researcher friend named Diane. We looked up and watched a shining silver disc, probably about fifty feet in diameter, fly halfway across the sky just under a layer of summer thunderclouds. It was right above us. It was travelling at about 100 mph and was perfectly visible below the snow white clouds and blue sky. We took little more notice of it than we would have of a jet fighter or oddly painted light plane flying over. We made a few casual remarks and comments about it and then continued our walk. I have heard over and over people saying, "If only I could see just one flying saucer!"

The Friendly Light

One late afternoon shortly after I took the "ice cube" photo I was driving out to the ranch. I usually tried to get there just before dark, so that I would have plenty of time to prepare any equipment I needed to get ready. The sun had set a half hour earlier so it was half-way between day and night. Linda and I learned early on that this was when the lights would often appear first. And it was often that it was when they were the most active. If they didn't appear then, then it would usually be several hours after sunset.

I drove through the ranch gate and soon came to the still usable, old two room adobe house in the front yard. Early settlers had built and abandoned the little house probably sometime in the 1920's. I pulled into my usual parking spot beside the adobe, when my eyes were instantly drawn to a light that was stationary in the sky above and behind the ranch house. I knew it probably wouldn't do any good to try to get a shot of it. My camera was in a pile with the other stuff in the back, and by the time I got it out the light would be gone. So I just sat in the van and stared at the light. Lights usually weren't out quite this early and I had never before seen one so close to the house, or in that particular location.

As I sat gazing at the light it began flashing in odd Morse code type sequences. This went on for a minute or so and then the light blinked out and was gone. This blinking on and out was their usual fashion. It was then that I suddenly realized that the pattern the light was flashing was exactly the pattern that Linda and I had been flashing to the lights the night before. That particular night before the lights had simply parked out there in the air with no return response at all. After I thought about it for a while, I said to myself that the damn things seem to even have a sense of humor. Pretty good joke, I thought.

I wish I could explicitly convey how awesomely strange and unusual some of these experiences have been for Linda, myself, and others. Truly, proper words fail miserably when I try to verbally draw a picture of many of these occurrences. One would have had to have been there. There are emotions, feelings and sensations one can't adequately express in words alone when witnessing something so out-of-the normal that the conscious and subconscious and the eyes grapple with a way to imprint the experience on the brain.

For instance: such as these next two experiences that each lasted no more than three seconds. One late night Linda was standing near and looking towards the bright kitchen light that Bob had just switched on. She did not see what took place behind her. I just happened to be facing in the right direction and saw it. I was about twenty steps away and looking toward Linda, when two bright flash camera like flashes lit up the immediate area where Linda stood. The two rapid flashes had come from above the top of a twenty-foot tall scrub oak just to my right. I chanced to be looking in that direction when the flashes took place. What is more interesting is that the source of the flash was clear light. It had no color to it whatsoever, but it flashed light which appeared white—like a flashbulb. Over the years I have seen so many enigmatic, anomalous episodes like this and I always wonder why. Why did it happen? What intelligence was behind it? What was the purpose? We weren't hurt so its intention wasn't injury to us. It was real. I saw it. But why—always, why?

This other three second episode is something that I feel some remorse about every time I think of it. One night during a profound and mystifying series of really strange (even to us) light episodes, I had gone into my van to reload my camera. This was my usual practice. I had in the van several flashlights with weak batteries. I could turn these on so as not to take an excessive chance on exposing film as I loaded it or unloaded it. I finished loading the film, and snapped shut the back of the eighteen-dollar point and shoot camera. I found that these, cheap, quick, manual cameras worked better than anything else.

Then another one of those brilliant ideas that seem to come out of nowhere pierced my thoughts. My back was to the two, open van side doors. I thought, and I remained there on my knees pondering this for a few moments - what if I spun around quickly and took a flash photo? I thought I might catch "something" invisible looking over my shoulder watching me load my camera. The green light on the back of my camera was on so I knew the camera's flash was powered up.

I spun around and quickly pressed the shutter button. The camera flash went off, and a millisecond later it was followed by a billowing fantasia like explosion of pure white light three feet in front of my face. Although the light explosion only lasted a few seconds it actually happened in slow motion. The flash explosion spread out to a diameter of about four feet. It had what resembled daisy petals that shot out from a center, then the "petals" drooped and then faded to blackness. After the shock wore off, I got the sad and definite feeling I had injured something very badly. The explosion of white light was a fantastically implausible sight. I now wish I hadn't done that, but how was I to know?

In conjunction with the last few light experiences are these. Sometimes Linda and I would walk around in the dark, usually after we ran out of film, with an unloaded camera and just keep triggering the flash. We wanted, just for the heck of it, to see if the flash would illuminate something we could not see. And it wasn't costing us rolls and rolls of film. Some of the things we saw were shadowy, black, unknown somethings moving at streaking speeds. Some were white. Linda was good at this. She could catch them time after time and interestingly, there were many times when Linda and I both clearly saw an object in front of a loaded camera after a flash, but the object did not show up on the film at all.

One night, with loaded cameras, Linda and I chanced to flash our cameras simultaneously in the same direction. We were about forty feet apart. For several seconds we saw a perfect, solid white, curved feather which was suspended vertically in the air and was about ten feet off the ground. The feather like object was about thirty feet in front of us. The feather was about four feet long. Again, what and why? It was there, and the last thing on earth we were both thinking of was a four-foot long white feather.

Dinosaurs From Another Time Or Dimension

One dead calm night in the summer of 1996, I had just reloaded my camera and was walking back to where I had been. Linda came over to me with an uncharacteristic look of exasperation on her face and said, or rather demanded, "Didn't you hear me?!" I stopped, looked at her in complete puzzlement, paused and replied simply, "No ... why?"

As it turned out Linda had been standing not more than fifty feet from me out in the open field. This was while I was in the van, side doors wide open toward her, reloading my camera. It seems she had seen two dinosaurs, the plant-eating types with huge bodies, long beefy tails and long snake like necks—diplodocus. She said the dinosaurs were feeding on low bushes and noticed her immediately after she saw them. They were about a hundred and fifty yards away. They raised their towering necks to full height to look at her. That's when she got a little panicky, and was shouting at me to come over and look—quick!

I didn't hear her—at all. She could have talked to me in a normal voice from that distance and I would have clearly heard her. I know she really had had the experience by how excited she was over it. The only thing we could figure was that Linda had somehow, temporarily been in another time or dimension. During the swampy Mesozoic era, prehistoric Arizona was full of dinosaurs of many kinds. Arizona has some of the richest fossil beds in the world.

I might add that, along these same lines, one night Linda was out by herself. She later told me that something, a creature, quite large, hissed in her face. Reptiles do that. She said that whatever it was she couldn't see it. It was invisible.

I have discussed many of my encounters, and Linda's encounters, with men and women who are tops in the paranormal publishing and research business. And, even they sometimes stare at me blankly and shake their heads. Even they, or many like them anyway, have never run across the kinds of paranormal experiences I have had personally. I'd sure like to know the why of this. Someone said to me a couple of years ago, "It's because you believe in them that you see them." Yeah, well—maybe.

I really do hope that at least a few people have some doors opened for them out of what I write. One of those few people might just nail this whole thing right on the head—for all of us. And, I think, what I write about here will be every day common experience, in the future.

Two Red Spheres

Sometimes, it seems, I am the only one in the vicinity who can physically see paranormal anomalies. The following are examples of this. In October of 1997, I drove to a spot I had not been to before. It seemed it might be a good place to observe more of the lights I had been chasing and photographing for so long. It was just off the Cornville Road near Highway 89-A. On the rather secluded spot that I went to is now an eighteen-hole golf course and a spreading wasteland of upscale houses.

Clouds were gathering when I left Sedona, and by the time I got to the spot it was looking more and more like rain. I drove off the highway following a cow path road for a few hundred yards. I deliberated about what to do, stay, or turn around and drive the fifteen miles back to Sedona. Rain drops were spattering on my windshield and several times I had to turn on the wipers to clear the windshield.

The clouds by now completely blacked out the stars, and the darkening rain clouds had lowered to a thousand feet above ground level. I was absentmindedly staring out through the windshield not really thinking about anything. I had chalked up the night as a loss as visibility was dropping by the minute. It looked like a hard rain was imminent.

The very next moment, I found myself watching a developing sight that utterly electrified my whole being, body and soul.

I was riveted to my space. I was now wide-eyed and barely breathing at what I was seeing. Not more than a half mile away, a luminous, crimson-red sphere, about a hundred feet in diameter was slowly emerging out of the underneath of a black storm cloud. By then my mouth was open in sheer disbelief. I glanced all around. That huge brightly glowing object was in full view of the entire city of Cottonwood. A city of eighteen thousand people (this includes the "suburbs"). I thought that this was incredible! This time one of these things would—finally!—be seen by thousands of people around here!

The glowing red sphere was composed of many seemingly living, blazing, colors but the dominant color was red. So it basically looked red. The sphere just hung there for a while—a hundred feet or so underneath the black cloud. The sphere started to move and at about thirty mph it flew right over Verde Village, east of Cottonwood's 9,800 people.

Had I had a low light video camera then (few affordable ones existed then) I could have easily taken film footage that would have kept the skeptics screaming and debating for years. The film would have been an instant sensation everywhere. A still camera tracking a moving nighttime object is worthless. The object develops as a badly blurred erratic mass. Water over the falls.

The sphere continued on, rose in altitude up to the Mingus Ridge, and then drifted through a gap in the mountain and was gone.

Seconds before the first one went out of sight, ANOTHER ONE came down out of the clouds near where the first one had appeared! The second one was identical to the first. I watched in complete rapture and awe as this one also swept across the valley. But this one, instead of going over the mountains, followed for miles below the black outline of Mingus Ridge. Then, it also flew through a gap on the ridge. I thought that this thing must have been seen by anyone outside or driving a car. It was unavoidable not to see it.

I thought that the next day would be one of chaos as crowds gathered around the Verde Valley to talk about what they had seen the night before. All the local newspapers would be full of interviews and photos taken by eye witnesses.

But nothing! Absolutely nothing!!!

If anyone besides me had seen those things, they didn't talk. As far as I know not a word was ever said by another person. You would have had to have been there to see those red orbs.

The Imposing Black Object

Here is the second example. On March 15°, 1998, between 6:30 p.m. and 6:45 p.m., almost exactly a year after the now famous "Lights over Phoenix" episode, I had an experience similar in scope to the red spheres over Cottonwood sighting. (At the time I was standing in the Rodeway Inn parking lot on Buckeye Road in Phoenix.) I was waiting for my psychologist friend, Tom O'Donnell, to arrive from Alaska. I was at the entrance to Sky Harbor International Airport. I was casually watching airliners landing on my right and left, as they flew low over downtown Phoenix on their approach pattern to the airport that was behind me.

As I was watching an airliner coming in over downtown Phoenix, I saw something unusual. It looked like what I first thought was a large, black helicopter. It was following close behind the airliner. I thought, Damn! That's dangerous! The black object was no more than two hundred yards behind the airliner and was off to the airliner's left (or west) a bit. After about a half mile of being right behind the airliner, the "helicopter" peeled off and flew directly northeast. Then after a few more miles, the object made a 90 degree turn and came straight in my direction. As it came closer I could see that it was no helicopter. It was an absolutely black object about fifty feet in diameter (it could have been much larger). The main body of the craft or ship or whatever it was was egg-shaped. It had two spike-like protrusions about twenty feet long, one on the top and one on the bottom. These spikes were somewhat cone-shaped, as they were wider where they attached to the craft. On its sides spaced evenly apart were three, maybe twenty foot long rods with large round balls on each end. If the craft really was about fifty feet in diameter, then these balls would have been eight feet or so in diameter.

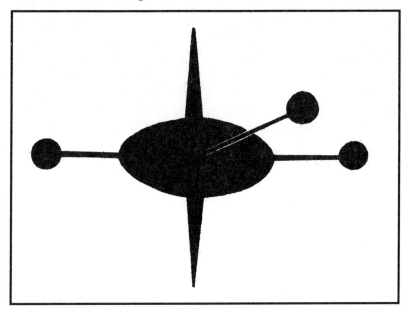

By now I had my binoculars out and got a clear, close-up look at the craft. I have to vigorously emphasize that this thing was the blackest black of anything I have ever seen. I have never seen anything that could begin to compare with it. It was absolute black, flat black, and no light reflected off it. Do I think it was something evil, or demonic, or satanic because it was absolute black? My answer is no.

This thing was in clear line of sight of millions of people. I had not watched this thing for two or three seconds, but for fifteen solid minutes. Perhaps my focused concentration on the object was somehow detected by it, because immediately prior to its departure I received a strange feeling of being "scanned" by it. As it passed over the area where I stood, it turned 90 degrees again, went straight up and in minutes disappeared vertically into a hazy, high altitude cloud layer almost directly above me.

I thought about it for about five minutes and then made a dash for the closest payphone. I called Sky Harbor International Airport and they straight away connected me to the main office. I asked, and they replied that they had no unusual blips or reports of loose balloons, out of place planes, helicopters or anything else. The thing had not shown up on radar. I did not have a camera with me that day. I was sure they would blow me off as just another whacked out crackpot making a drug crazed or crank call. But instead, to my pleasant surprise, they treated me with earnest respect and took my report with dead, no fooling seriousness. Go figure. Did they know something they weren't telling me? As far as I know no one else but me saw that object. Again, why? Who? Why me?

CHAPTER SEVEN

Places To Look For The Sedona Lights

The majority of the local flying, or stationary, mystery light phenomena occurs in the open deserts surrounding Sedona. But these lights can be encountered just about anywhere in the entire Verde Valley. This includes the cities, towns and settlements of Sedona, Cottonwood, Clarkdale, Jerome, Camp Verde, the Village of Oak Creek, Lake Montezuma, Montezuma Well, Cornville and Childs. This is an area of hundreds of square miles. Childs is a tiny four building hydroelectric facility constructed in the 1930's. It is in the remote lower end of the Verde Valley on the Verde River. The valley there is almost U-shaped and the valley sides are precipitous. Childs had a UFO flap in the late 1980's that is still being talked about today. It remains one of the world's most intense UFO flaps.

Actually, as far as the lights are concerned, the area immediately to the west of Jerome on the Mingus Ridge has, over the years, been the single most active area for these lights. But this area is also quite remote, and the lights here are often only seen from a vantage point many miles away out on the flats.

People ask me where is the best place and time locally to go and watch for these mysterious lights. I always reply that it can be anywhere, anytime of the year. There is absolutely no consistent pattern to the appearance of these lights—and UFO's. The best single place to go to watch for these lights at night is anywhere in the general vicinity of the junction of Boynton Pass Road and the Red Canyon Road. A mile or two in any direction of this junction is also good. Another good spot is the Red Canyon Road halfway to Hwy 89-A. This whole area is about six miles driving distance from Sedona.

And incidentally, as I have said in many of my other writings, if someone gets a really awesome photograph—or already has one, write to me at the address at the back of the book. I will either trade a photo of comparable value, or return your photo. I will add it to a collection that I do not keep for profit and is always open to serious researchers.

At the time of this writing both Boynton Pass Road and Red Canyon Road are rough (in dry weather easily driven by car) gravel, desert roads. However, if developers have their way (the area is already "developed"—it's got trees on it!) it will in a few years be a wide two lane paved highway complete with painted stripes down the middle. And, yet another eighteen-hole golf course and hundreds of time shares are proposed for that area. This is what is called progress.

When I moved to Sedona in 1986 there were just a few thousand people living here. There were about a million tourists a year. Now in 1999 the population is over 17,000 and there are over four million tourists who come here every year. It is also estimated that soon, during the course of a year, a million time share holders will temporarily live here. Sedona, California? Scottsdale North? Santa Fe West?

The Ten Foot White Sphere

This next incident is one of the rarest that I know of because it happened right in the center of Sedona at ground level. A local man had just picked up his girlfriend from work at a local restaurant. She was a waitress. It was April 15, 1997 at about 9:00 p.m. They lived on upper Andante Street. They were driving halfway up Andante, when a ten foot high sphere of bright white light came out of a side street (left) and stayed just ahead of their van for about a half block. Then the light turned right on to Arrowhead Road (East). All the while the light was only a few feet above the pavement.

After the light turned right it went only a short way, then rose up into the night sky and streaked over Coffee Pot Rock a mile away. The whole episode lasted less than seven seconds. Always looking for corroboration, I asked around and quickly located a man who was out walking his dog at the time. He is a local desert, tour guide. He saw the light rise up into the sky near Andante Street. Then he watched as the light streaked at a fantastic speed over Coffee Pot Rock. Three witnesses from two totally different vantage points.

The man and the young woman who saw the light go up Andante also had a strange light sighting later, in June of 1997. They described how to the east of Sedona they watched five red lights appear high in the night sky. Then, a huge white sphere next appeared, split in two, and then all the lights flew away in different directions. Quite rapidly.

Over the past twenty years this has been a rather common occurrence over Schnebly Hill to the northeast of Sedona. It's always red lights and white lights, and the pattern of appearance and disappearance is almost always different. There have been dozens of these types of sightings. One of these red and white light incidents in 1993 was seen by at least a hundred people in downtown Sedona. I was told that the sighting was spectacular. I talked to an out-of-town businessman who had watched the whole thing from his hotel room that faced Schnebly Hill. From what he said, an enormous white glowing sphere appeared at the top of Schnebly Hill about five miles away. In slow motion five smaller red spheres emerged from it and when all five were out, all the lights streaked away each in a different direction. Again, this was seen by as many as a hundred people. Maybe more.

Two Alaska Bush Pilots And The Silver Ball

Many Sedona area UFO and light sightings involve one or more eminently credible witnesses. This next incident is one of the best. On June 30', 1997 two women who were both Alaska bush pilots were flying in a single engine plane over the Beaver Creek area east of Sedona. They were about one mile west of the Beaver Creek Ranger Station. The woman who was flying the plane had a reputation as being one of the best bush pilots in Alaska. No small feat for anyone—man or woman.

June 30' of 1997 was a bright, clear, cloudless day. Suddenly, from far below the plane, a blazingly bright basketball sized sphere of silver light rose up out of an arroyo and came alongside the plane. The woman said the brightly luminous ball stayed with them for a minute or two. They explained that the silver ball seemed to be very interested in them and/or the small aircraft. Then the silver object changed direction, and in seconds disappeared over the Mogollon Rim to the north.

The next day, a dead horse was found less than a half mile from where the silver sphere shot out of the arroyo. I didn't see the horse myself, but a friend of mine who is an experienced researcher from Phoenix did see it. He is the same fellow who had personally interviewed the two women pilots. He told how the whole thing with the horse was damn strange. He said the dead yearling horse did not fit the usual cattle or horse mutilation scenario, but he said the horse had puncture wounds on its body that were not bullet wounds. And the horse was not cut up. Another thing that struck me as odd was that I have never seen horses in that particular area.

The Curious Orange Light

In the fall of 1996 Linda Bradshaw and four other local people had a most unusual encounter. On a whim one evening, they had decided to get together several days later for a night time bonfire at the hangman's gallows. The gallows are on a nearby hill behind the old western town movie set. Over the years a number of Hollywood desperadoes got their necks stretched through the trap door of those gallows.

They got a roaring bonfire going and were enjoying the lovely evening and the panorama of the surrounding desert and hills. It was the first night of a full moon. When, off to the northeast in the direction of Sedona an orange sphere was seen low over the desert. As the group focused their attention on the light, the light began moving in their direction. The light continued to come closer and closer and came to within several hundred feet of the group and stopped. This entire episode was videotaped, but when the tape was later played back the tape was completely blank.

The orange light seemed to be curious about the fire and

was probably drawn by the bright fire. It hovered there for some minutes, then blinked out. At the same time the orange sphere blinked out, the faintly glowing outline of a disc-shaped craft about thirty feet across was suddenly visible at the bottom of a sandy wash in the arroyo below the hill. The glowing outline very slowly began to rise vertically off the dry sandbar. Shortly it was at eye level with the group. Then, abruptly, there was a blinding flash and the "ship" streaked away to the northeast. A good skeptic would respond, "Sure! They were just seeing some sort of reflection from the fire—or the planet Venus!" Some glowing swamp gas maybe?

Ok, well how about this. There was a man that night who had elected to stay at the ranch house instead of going to the bonfire. This man saw the "ship" streak past the ranch house and disappear over Loy Butte to the northeast. Maybe four people could have a vivid hallucination or shared delusion, but how could a fifth who had no idea what had transpired be a crucial eyewitness to a critical part of the event? In short—it happened.

Here are two other light incidents I had almost forgotten about, but are of great significance. One night in 1997 Linda and I were out in an open field doing our routine photo flashing. Linda had recently purchased a new, state of the art camcorder. This was at the very tail end of our research activities.

A white light appeared in the distance and Linda tried to video tape the light. We finally gave up on that camera as we soon discovered it was useless in low light conditions. At any rate, the light did not appear on the played back tape, but what did show up on the film was a red beam of light that swept back and forth across the lens. The white light, or something, was scanning us.

On another occasion, much later, Linda did finally videotape a light. It is, in my opinion, an amazing video. This small white light followed Linda closely as she walked around outside the ranch house. It came to within about sixty feet of her. Her commentary is also on the tape as this is transpiring. You can actually see this six inch or so light moving around through bushes and little pine trees as it followed Linda. I believe this transpired for ten minutes or more. It was a brightly shining little light.

My Cornville Light Ship Encounter

This story is in some ways similar to the orange bonfire light incident. Over the Christmas holidays in 1996, I was house-sitting a friend's house in Cornville.

One night several days after my friend had gone back to New York, I was walking past an upstairs window. I could not help but notice a strange light in the direction of "downtown" Cornville. The light was so bright it resembled the landing light on a single engine aircraft. But it was not fully dark yet. It would not be fully dark for another hour.

I stood in the window carefully watching the light. By now, I knew the light was not normal. All of my research equipment (except a pair of Megan's binoculars which by then I had in my hand) was down in my van. From long experience I knew if I took the time to run for my camera, when I got back the object would be gone. So, I thought I might as well stay where I was and see what would happen.

The light drifted in my direction slowly. There was still daylight enough so that I could see houses miles away. It's a mostly flat area with a few rolling hills. The bright lights' point of origin was precisely over Casey's Corner. This was about two miles from where I stood. The now incredibly bright light came to about three hundred yards from me and then stopped. As it hovered, it gave me time to use Megan's powerful binoculars, to really focus in on it. In the center of the light was a form that looked like a mercurial silver eye. Everything was there, round iris, pupil, eyeball shape—everything. At times the "eye" would change colors. At times it looked like a navy blue color instead of shiny silver. I stood there watching this thing thinking of all the things I have seen over the years. What next? This one was new to me. I had never seen anything to compare to it.

As I watched, mesmerized through the binoculars, the light blinked off. I lowered the binoculars. In the place where the light had been was now a silver disc-shaped craft.

It seemed to be about twenty feet in diameter. The "craft" was perfectly disc-shaped but had a slight bump-like protrusion on the top half. I got a perfect look at the ship—or whatever it was. I inspected it for about ten seconds. Then, like the light before it, it simply blinked out and was gone.

I remained where I was staring at the general area where the ship had been. Trying to make some sense out of just another weird, eerie, supernatural, mystical, enigmatic, fathomless, bewildering event.

Not more than five minutes after the ship had blinked out, I saw a single engine light plane approaching low in the distance. Way too low. It had its steady burning red light and flashing white strobe light on. When the "light plane" came to near where the craft had first appeared over Casey's Corner, the small plane began to make half mile wide circles around the area. "What the hell!" I exclaimed to myself. That plane was flying so damn low (it was now much darker out but I could still make out houses in the distance), I was amazed one of the wings didn't clip the top of a tree, or the top of a hill, or a telephone wire. I wondered what the folks at Casey's Corner must have thought about the plane circling so low. The "plane" circled in different, wider and narrower patterns at least ten times, then flew away to the northeast. More Questions. Where did that plane come from so quickly? Where did it originate from? What drew it there and/or who sent it there? Was it after what I had seen? If it was a government aircraft how did it get there so fast? Had it not been for the appearance of the light plane, I would have wondered if I had not created somehow, or imagined the whole light/ship sighting in its entirety.

Binky Story

This following story has nothing to do with Sedona but by its extreme nature it lends credibility to this book with its unusual incidents, encounters and occurrences. Hence my reason to include it.

It involves my friend Tom O'Donnell. I asked Tom if he wanted his name used with this story, and he insisted that I do so—further lending credibility to the incident. I am sure this ties in—somehow—with everything I have written about in this book. It happened just in time to be included here.

Tom and I have been willing, and sometimes unwilling, associates in a paranormal scenario that has transpired since we became friends thirteen years ago. Strange—and I mean strange—things have happened particularly when Tom and I are in the same place at the same time. I suppose in some before—this—current—life we agreed to be part of some larger picture I for one certainly can't begin to explain or understand.

On the evening of February 13˚, 2000 about 8:00 p.m., Tom went outside to get something out of his car. It was raining lightly and a nearby streetlight lit up the surrounding area. Tom lives in a quiet neighborhood in southern California. His constant companion Binky, a Yorkshire Terrier, went out with him. It was one of the very few times Binky was not on a leash. Tom was rummaging around in his car and after a few seconds remembered the dog. He looked up in time to see Binky headed for the road. A car was coming.

Binky walked into the street and the car ran over him. The driver had heard and felt the thump under his tires, and had seen Tom running toward the street waving his arms as he tried to catch Binky.

The new Binky.

The driver, a young man, stopped the car, got out and walked back. The young man expressed great regret to the now completely distraught Tom. Tom had just lost his best friend. The little dog lay dead on the rain wet street. The street light clearly illuminated the gloomy scene.

The young man, now feeling extremely guilty and uncomfortable, again gave his regrets and got back into his car and drove away. It wasn't his fault or Tom's.

Tom stood over the dog for some minutes and became very emotional. Gathering himself, he went back inside to get a plastic bag to put Binky in. When he came back out just minutes later the dog was gone. He searched around, the body was gone. Not knowing what to do, Tom went back into the house. He called me on the phone in the meantime. I had never heard him so distraught and upset.

An hour went by. Tom heard a car drive up in front of his house. A door slammed and the car accelerated quickly away. Thinking that that was rather odd, Tom looked out through the curtains and then went over and opened the front door. And there was Binky, more alive and energetic than Tom had ever seen him. After a few moments of shock, relief and disbelief, Tom picked up Binky and brought him inside. There was not a scratch on the dog's body. The next day, Tom took Binky to a veterinarian and the vet after an examination, said the dog was completely normal. There were no bruises, cuts or broken bones.

Several things come to mind here. If the dog was not Binky but a replacement Yorkshire Terrier why did the dog run to Tom's door and was ecstatic to see Tom? And— who—really, was the driver of the first car—and the second car? Something of this magnitude of high strangeness must have an obvious purpose, but what?

The only other dog story—well documented and somewhat similar that I know of—was of an Indian family in South Dakota. An Indian man had died and afterward his beloved dog would not eat or drink. The dog was dying.

Early one evening, some people in the house saw the several days dead and buried man walk up to the front door and knock. Being Indians they were not shocked or terrified. The man stepped into the house and only said, "I've come back for my dog." The dog leaped to its feet and ran happily over to the man. Man and dog walked around a small knoll in front of the house and were never seen again.

Photo taken near Sedona in 1997 by Karne Snickers.

CHAPTER EIGHT

Can It Get Any Stranger Than This?

The Man With The Blue Hair

Just months after *Merging Dimensions* had been printed, Linda Bradshaw shot one of the most significant photographs ever taken by any person on this planet—ever. Six months after the photo was taken, it was included (free) in an interview that was filmed here in Sedona by a TV crew from a BBC affiliate in London.

This interview and several of my photographs and several of Linda's photographs were seen in 1998 coast to coast on *The Learning Channel*. The show re-ran six times. The interview was also shown on TV in Europe via the BBC.

Linda's photo shows a left side head profile and the left shoulder of a man with blue hair. I believe it is the first authentic photograph of an alien (or interdimensional) male ever taken. There have been several photos of alleged female aliens such as Billy Meier's photo of the blond female Pleiadian, Asket.

The Blue Haired Man's ear is different from ours. It is puffy and has no ear hole. Instead, it has only two small creases along its outer edge. In the profile of the head the left eye is so small that it is not visible. A normal human eye bulges out prominently when the profile is seen at the same angle. The Blue Haired Man is about seven and a half feet tall, judging from the angle of the camera. We came up with that figure because Linda took most of her shots holding her camera just above her head height. This was a random night flash photo. The Blue Haired Man was not visible to us, but appeared on the film negative.

There is an odd round mole-like growth directly in front

of the man's ear. Several MD's who looked at it said it almost appeared to be some sort of organ. Maybe a secondary ear organ—or it may indeed just be a mole.

The one thing that really strikes me as uncanny is the angled forward V shaped sideburn. Here's why. The sideburn is in all ways identical to the sideburns worn by James T. Kirk and the Enterprise crew from the original *Star Trek* series. This makes me wonder if Gene Roddenberry was privy to certain information before anyone else. The Blue Haired Man looks to be about thirty-five years old—in human terms. He may be a thousand years old in terms of some other race or system. Paradoxically, he is wearing what looks to be a standard, run-of-the-mill, blue athletic sweatsuit top with a blue flap-down hood.

Linda and I were standing side-by-side when she took the Blue Haired Man photograph. We were the only ones in the vicinity. The man's head is now centered in the photo and is

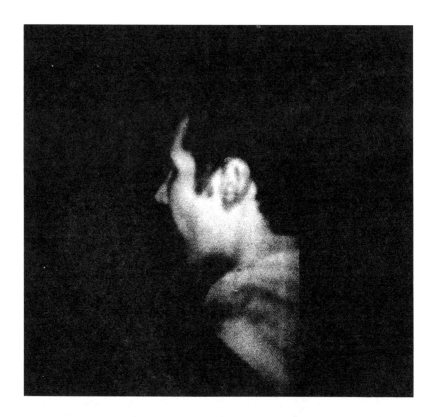

cut off a bit in the back. The reason for that is that the head was at the extreme right of the negative. The negative was pulled to the left so that the man's head would now be in the center of the print. The back of his head is not flat, his head was originally at the very edge of the negative.

I know that disbelievers and skeptics would jump up and down and scream their brains out, Hoax! Hoax! Hoax! I've heard it before. But whatever my integrity and credibility are worth I can attest that the Blue Haired Man photo is not a hoax in any shape, manner or form.

The critical question that remains is—Who is he?

The Sandal Foot Photo

On the back cover of *Merging Dimensions* is the photograph of, up until a year ago, what we thought was a very small unidentified flying object. It's a shot I took. Because of grass and small flowers near it, we think the mysterious object is about ten inches wide and ten inches tall.

A few years ago I had taken a few negatives to a photo shop in uptown Sedona. The technician wasn't clear on what I wanted and enlarged the wrong section of the negative. But ... as I gazed disappointedly at the finished prints, I noticed two sandaled feet in one of the blow-ups. "What's this!" I exclaimed in the shop. I examined the 5X8 inch photo more closely and sure enough, there were two feet with sandals on them in the bottom of the photo. I had them blow up the whole left side of the negative into a 5X8 and even more astonishing details showed up.

The toes were rather odd. They are bigger and rounder than normal. And above the feet is a long, blue, baggy pant leg that ends at a huge potbelly—or a massive chest—it's hard to tell. There is a right arm and where the right hand should be is what we once thought was a UFO. That was before the accidental wrong blow-up.

The object is obviously not a UFO, but is some sort of device the being is holding in his right hand. Or—the device could BE his right hand. Unfortunately, no head is visible in the photo.

There are two other fascinating aspects to this photo. One is that it was a bitter cold winter night in mid-

February. Bare feet in sandals?

Aspect number two is that the being, or person, was not visible to human eyes, but the legs cast an obvious shadow on the ground. I could not see the being but he, she, or it, had enough density to cast a shadow. Eyes could not see the being but the being registered on film. What was the device in its hand. A weapon? An illumination device? A detector of some sort? Could it be a device that kept the being invisible to a human? I for one would absolutely love to know. And, is the being in the sandals the Blue Haired Man?

Thirty-eight Photos

In 1996—again right after *Merging Dimensions* was printed, an elusive and mystifying event was transpiring in-

side the Bradshaw's ranch house. If there hadn't been so many mind-bending super-paranormal goings-on at the ranch, this incident would have been hard to believe. Even for me. But it happened. Here is how it went.

Linda would leave her camera on the coffee table, in the kitchen, or where ever. She always took note of how many exposures were left on the roll at the end of the day. The next morning the camera would still be where she had left it. But instead of, say, ten exposures on the film counter—it would now have fifteen or more showing in the little window on the camera. This sort of thing went on for a long time.

One night Linda fell asleep on the living room sofa. "Somebody" during the night had picked up the camera and had taken a panorama photo of the living room. About six separate photos in all if I remember correctly. All but where Linda was sleeping on the sofa. We soon deduced that the photos were being taken from three feet off the floor. All thirty-eight photos taken by the "somebody" were taken from about three feet off the floor. So the somebody would have been about four feet tall—or less.

At the time, this was at the pinnacle of paranormal activity at the ranch. We figured it couldn't get any crazier than this. It was the frosting on the cake. This capped it off. After a while we developed a sense of humor about everything that was happening to us and around us, and again, we were never hurt in any way.

Late one evening, a bunch of us were sitting around the kitchen table at the ranch, when another brilliant idea suddenly flashed in my brain. I pondered it for a second then burst out with, "Hey. Let's dust the camera with baby powder tonight and see what happens!" Everybody looked at each other and replied in unison that they thought it was a great idea. That night Linda dusted her camera all over, liberally, with baby powder and put the camera out in plain view on the coffee table.

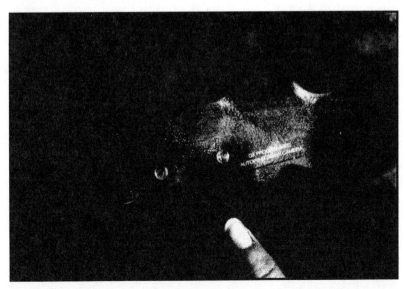

That very night, the being or creature—whatever—picked the camera up, took one photo and sat the camera back down. It never took another. And, it made no attempt to clean the camera. It left two perfect "finger" prints on the camera. One print was on the left side of the camera and is far larger than a normal human fingerprint. The print on the left side of the camera was about an inch wide, an inch long and almost square. The print on the top of the camera looks like the "finger" may have had a claw on it. And, the top print was fuzzy as if the finger was covered in soft, dense fur. Another possibility is that the creature's hand was not completely materialized into physicality.

And yet again, the demanding question is, who was he, or her, or it?!

What I have written here—in this book—as wildly beyond the normal as most of it is ... as I said earlier could this all become perfectly normal activity in our future?

Sai Baba Too!

During the height of all the high strangeness at the Bradshaw Ranch, about a half dozen Sai Baba related events also occurred. These events occurred in divergent forms at different times. If you aren't familiar with who Sai Baba is, he currently resides in India and is—probably—the last living genuine Avatar. Sai Baba is credited with doing everything that Jesus did, including bringing a person who has died back to life—and completely healing those with hopeless illnesses and afflictions. Some of these miraculous healings were witnessed by traditional medical doctors.

Linda is a Sai Baba devotee—as am I. At the ranch Linda had a Sai Baba room with an altar with various Sai Baba related goods on it. There were large photos of Sai Baba in his orange robes, a canister of vibuti, some incense, some crystals, and some other things I can't recall. The canister of vibuti was pint sized and had a secure lid on it. Sai Baba materializes vibuti out of thin air. It is a powdery fine, gray, rose smelling and tasting ash. Linda would give it away freely to anyone who felt they needed it for a healing, for inspiration, or whatever. The jar in time was almost empty. Those of us who are familiar with Sai Baba's documented miracles have heard the following story many times. Sai Baba—or someone—seems to keep track of vibuti in personal quantities around the world and sometimes, mysteriously, refills empty vibuti containers.

One day Linda opened her almost empty jar of vibuti and, to her amazement, the jar was now brim full. And—on the surface of the smooth, packed vibuti was the clear, impressed image of a lotus flower. The lotus flower has for thousands of years been the calling card of Avatars. So is the odor of fresh roses when they are nearby either physically or mentally. On at least six occasions Linda and I while outside doing our photo sleuthing would detect the strong, sweet smell of roses on the breeze. Even in the dead of winter. The sudden aroma of roses in a room, or wherever, has often been the signature of the direct or indirect presence of a great Christed Avatar.

Down through history tales of rooms suddenly filling with the fragrance of roses has been often acknowledged as the presence of an Avatar (and others). Sai Baba, and others, have said that you will know when I am there by the aroma of roses. Even if they were many thousands of miles away.

I'd like to know how they do that.

Dada-Ji, a relatively unknown Indian master also signaled his presence by the smell of roses—in many ways. Dada-Ji was one of the greatest Avatars who ever lived. But few have ever even heard his name. He did not seek attention. Dada-Ji died in India in 1996. He was 82.

So, perhaps Sai Baba kept an eye on Linda and I during all those strange, confusing and other worldly times. To this day I have no idea what Sai Baba's interest in us was. At least twice a month during a particular stretch in 1995-96 someone would come sheepishly to the ranch door and say something like, "I hope you don't think I'm crazy, but I felt I had to come here ... and bring this vibuti (or a new photo of Sai Baba). I am a follower of Sai Baba." The first few times this happened it was roundly confusing for everyone. After a while a pattern, or a picture, began to emerge.

One day a visibly nervous couple knocked at the ranch house door. Bob, who is a tall, lean, stern looking Arizona cowboy—cowboy boots, blue jeans, belt buckle, cowboy shirt, red neckerchief, cowboy hat and all came to the door. He is a good natured guy with a wry sense of humor. Before the now more nervous than ever couple said anything Bob asked, "Who sent you?" With trepidation the lady replied, "Sai Baba." She probably expected to get shot. Bob opened the door wide and said in a welcoming tone of voice, "Why, come right on in!" Even Bob was getting used to it all by then. In time we ended up with about nine slightly different kinds of vibuti out of all this. Every visitor brought vibuti and we mixed it all together. I still have a pouch of it that goes with me everywhere I go. It's one of my proudest possessions.

The event that topped this all off though was one that I still marvel at and always will. It begins with an American woman who lives in Italy. She is a devout follower of Sai Baba. She told us that one night Sai Baba materialized in front of her in her home in Italy. He said to her that she must go immediately to Sedona, Arizona. Then without more to say, Sai Baba dematerialized. Sedona, Arizona!!! She had to look it up on a map. The woman was totally perplexed by this. It would be exceedingly difficult for her to leave at this time. Her husband was an Italian who was in big business in that country, and he heavily relied on her knowledge at the office.

The next day, on an impulse, she called a woman friend of hers who lives in northern Florida. Almost immediately, after hearing the story she excitedly replied to her friend in Italy, "You are not going to believe this but a Buddist monk was just here. He told me I had to leave right away and go to the Bradshaw Ranch in Sedona, Arizona!" Then the monk left. The two women were almost beside themselves with incredulity.

After making some difficult arrangements with her husband, the woman in Italy, within hours, was on a plane to Florida. The two women then flew on to Arizona. Both women logically assumed that the Bradshaw Ranch was an ashram, or some kind of spiritual community or retreat. When they arrived in Sedona they were shocked to learn that the Bradshaw Ranch was just a standard, nuts and bolts, working Arizona cattle ranch. They figured they had come that far, so when they got out to the ranch they were told all the other Sai Baba stories. They felt better. Much better.

The two women, Linda and I and several friends, stayed up half the first night trying to make some heads or tails of it all.

We never did figure it out, but the two women had a wonderful time at the ranch, and Linda and I ended up with a marvelous collection of vibuti.

Maybe everyone who came there, seen or unseen, brought something special with them for some reason we may never understand.

I guess only Sai Baba knows what the ultimate reason for it all was. We will probably never know.

Not in this life anyway.

Commentary: Tom Dongo's Sedona

by Tom O'Donnell, Ed.D.

I met Tom under somewhat mysterious circumstances, back in the mid-1980s. I was a psychologist in Florida at the time, and knew nothing of Sedona, UFO's, or other matters paranormal. It was just not part of my philosophy. Since meeting Tom, we have maintained a close friendship even though I have usually lived many thousands of miles from his Sedona residence. But whether it was during the years spent working with the Eskimos in Alaska, or with the Conch citizens in the Florida Keys, a week has not passed without an exchange. Whenever possible I would fly into Arizona and spend several days with him, becoming acquainted with his latest investigation. In the next several pages I would like to share with the reader a few of the more outstanding, truly remarkable recollections of my time spent with Tom Dongo. These are stories that Tom has not shared with you in any of his books. Frankly, he has experienced so many extraordinary events since coming to Sedona that only a sampling can be presented in his written works.

First, several words are in order as to the unusual manner of our meeting. In 1987 I had a remarkable dream in which I heard a voice tell me to go to a place called Sedona. I hadn't heard of this place, and actually had to consult a map to see where this "Sedona" was located, if indeed there were a place by this name. Of course I confirmed that it was in Arizona. Due to the unusual nature of the dream, I decided to act upon it and fly out for a visit. I had no plans other than to go there and see what developed, if anything. After arriving I began studying a bulletin board at a visitor's center to get hints on what to do. I focused in on Tom's card, and knew intuitively I was to meet this man. His card at the time was offering customized tours of Sedona. I thus enrolled in "Sedona 101," which included an introduction to the vortices sites such as found in Boynton Canyon. I was immediately impressed with Tom's common sense, low-keyed, even downright humble manner. He has proven as genuine now as when I first met him nearly fourteen years ago.

After that initial visit I took a respite from my Florida practice about every other month, flying in to share in Tom's investigative research into the paranormal.

I would like to share with the reader a very different kind of experience I had with Tom back in the early 1990s. It is by far and away the most incredible week I ever spent with this gifted clairvoyant investigator.

The setting is rural Minnesota; the time is Summer, 1992. It is past midnight, with a full moon's light threatening to expose Tom and I and an accomplice as we dig frantically in a farmer's field, looking for a corpse that we *knew* had been buried there. I know, this sounds like the grave robber scene from *Frankenstein*. I'd better back up a bit and explain.

Several weeks earlier I had come across a flyer having a photo of a boy who had been abducted in rural Minnesota. Coincidentally, the abduction occurred not far from the most famous child abduction in U.S. history—the 1930's Lindbergh baby abduction. As with the Lindbergh case, the present day abduction had received national attention. Of course, a plethora of clairvoyants and mediums had tried their hands at finding the boy but, up to that point, to no avail. As soon as I saw this flyer I intuitively knew that Tom could find the child. I just *knew* it. Or at least I thought he could tell the parents if the boy were alive or dead. From experience I was aware that Tom was particularly gifted in receiving detailed and accurate impressions on lost people, lost pets, and lost belongings. In fact, we had done a number of experiments in remote viewing in 1990 and 1991 which demonstrated Tom's ability to project his awareness to designated places, and report accurately what was going on there. I had estimated his accuracy level to exceed 80 percent in those experiments.

Tom somewhat surprised me when he agreed to fly to

Minnesota and spend a week in an effort to solve the abduction mystery. We had little to go on, other than reports
of where the boy was last seen. This lack of information actually pleased Tom, who preferred to obtain his impressions free of potentially biasing information. So we began
to drive around the Minnesota country-side. While driving
I would ask questions as Tom utilized a technique he developed over the years to help pick up a trail. Kind of like a
hunting dog can do with a scent. He described the technique in terms of sending out a wave of energy. He would
then examine the returning echoes for relevant impressions. It sounded to me similar to the way radar works.

Several days went by, with hundreds of miles driven, but
no promising findings were received. On the third day,
however, we thought we hit pay dirt. Tom suddenly began
receiving very strong impressions as we drove through a
certain rural area. They were not positive. In fact, on several occasions I thought he would be overwhelmed by
them. He even began to groan as he saw in his mind certain scenes. There were visual impressions of an organized
band of child abductors and molesters that, we ultimately
discovered, may encompass several Midwest states. To
make matters worse, a bizarre religious flavor seemed present in the predators' activities. Those involved had developed rituals which could only be described as pathologi-
cally demented. Tom also received impressions that some
of those involved in this activity were actually respected citizens of their communities. Talk about a double life! (Author's note: At that time, I got impressions on a ring based
in northern Iowa that was kidnapping children throughout
the midwest. This later turned out to be 100% correct.)

While driving down a back road on the fourth day, Tom's
"radar" began going wild. He zeroed in on a vacant field,
behind a decrepit farmhouse. He felt sure that there was a
body buried in that field. He also received very unsettling
impressions of the person or persons residing in the house.

We did some checking in the community and found that
the man living in the house was considered quite strange.
Realizing that there was no way he would give us permis-
sion to investigate (*"Sir, could we dig up your back yard as we*

have a psychic impression that you buried a corpse there?"), we decided to let lapse our normally law-abiding ways. After midnight, we crept under the barbed wire fence with our shovels and, at the spot Tom felt to be "hottest," began to dig furiously. What happened next still baffles us, and in my opinion constitutes the best example of "high strangeness" I have to date experienced with Tom.

Down about three to four feet, I uncovered a glowing green ball—about the size of a marble. It was neither natural nor organic, such as a glow worm. It was a perfect orb with a brilliant, phosphorescent glow.   We looked at it briefly, dumbfounded, but for fear of being discovered we resumed our frantic digging. I was careful to put the orb in a secure pocket prepared to hold artifacts.

We dug further but found nothing else. We returned to the hotel and discussed the evening. I was certain Tom's "radar" detected something quite significant in that specific spot. He was certain as well. But we found no bones, no bits of clothing—nothing that we were fearing to find.

Then, I remembered the green orb. I opened the snapped pocket but—it was gone. It could not have fallen out of the pocket as the container was secure. It simply vanished. And we were left with nothing but a good story.

It was toward the end of the week's search, while debriefing each other over a couple of beers, that Tom suddenly received the impression that ET's were somehow involved in this whole thing. Perhaps they were monitoring our efforts. Or, perhaps they were more involved. I suspect that the green orb we uncovered may have been placed in the spot to draw Tom's psychic attention. How else could something so strange have gotten there, right at the location which captured Tom's psychic attention. But why? For what purpose? Tom did receive the additional impression that we came very, very close to uncovering a dark secret in rural Minnesota. But that there may have been forces that would have prevented us from getting any closer. Perhaps karmic issues needed to be played out and resolved—free from interference of two meddling outsiders. Tom later received confirmation from a law enforcement agency, active in the abduction case, that some of his impressions were uncannily accurate—reflecting details that were previously documented in the case but not publicly known. At least some satisfaction was derived from this knowledge. But, as is so typical of investigations into high strangeness, the end result was not at all what was anticipated.

In Tom's investigations, it seems that more questions are raised than answers. Initially, I had hoped, even expected that answers would be forthcoming. I was naive. It doesn't seem to work that way, does it? In Tom's series of books, the theme of *producing more questions than answers* frequently surfaces. I believe there is an inclination for many investigators and authors to cough up explanations that are not well supported. When an author does come up with a preponderance of answers, my intuition tells me to "Go elsewhere!"

After several years my initial eagerness and anticipation over Tom's paranormal investigations gave way to some disillusionment. I began to think, what was the point of Tom devoting his life to this full-time investigative effort? Yes, following Tom's work has been interesting for many of us, even fascinating on occasion but it has always been a financial burden on him. And the enlightening points can be few and far between. On several occasions he has called me and stated categorically that he is hanging it up—that it is time to get a real job and start living. Yet Tom Dongo continues on this quest, always raising more questions than answers. I can only conclude that arriving at the question is the real purpose of the quest. Perhaps expanding our consciousness has more to do with posing a question rather than producing an answer.

Author's Note

Because of the unusual content of this book, I thought it would be good to have perspectives on the book from several other people. I asked Chet Snow and Tom O'Donnell, two long-time friends whose opinions I highly value, to write their thoughts however they came and I would include them in this new book. My deepest thanks to them both.

However, I need to expand a bit on Tom O'Donnell's commentary. The kidnaping we worked on was the kidnaping of Jacob Wetterling.

Jacob at the time was eleven years old and he lived with his parents in St. Joseph, Minnesota. Tom and I both got very deeply involved in this case. Jacob would be about twenty years old now—if he is still alive. If anyone has any new information on Jacob Wetterling, please write to me at the address at the back of this book and I will forward it to the Jacob Wetterling Foundation.

That was a memorable night digging up that "grave" on the farmer's property. We had walked for quite a distance and came upon, right where I said it should be, what looked exactly like a year or so old grave. While digging up this "grave" I said to myself never—ever—would I do anything like this again. It was midnight in the middle of a hot, humid Minnesota summer. In minutes the three of us were dripping with sweat. We were in easy shotgun range of two farmhouses. A dog would bark occasionally. I've been shot at before—it's not a whole lot of fun.

When we were making a hasty getaway, near the road I walked into an electrified fence that felt like it had a million volts going through it. I let out a yell that could be heard for a long ways.

At any rate, I must have been close on many things I "saw" psychically in relation to the case. A month after returning from Minnesota I spent a congenial afternoon drinking lemonade at a table in my backyard with a very pleasant woman F.B.I. agent. We discussed the Jacob Wetterling case. She never did tell me *how* close I was to the F.B.I.'s own information, but I must have been accurate on many points—judging by the F.B.I.'s interest.

This book was finally printed during the second week of June, 2000. One week before the manuscript went to press, from a reliable source—a full-time pilot, I learned of a possible new network of tunnels and a possible underground (alien?) installation northeast of Page, Arizona on the Arizona, Utah border. This is a rugged and remote wilderness area. So far, this new information seems to have great substance. Too late to make this book, but the saga absolutely continues.

ORDERING BOOKS BY TOM DONGO
Autographed copies

__Everything You Wanted to Know
About Sedona In a Nutshell. . . . . $4.95 $_____

__Merging Dimensions . . . . $14.95 $_____

MYSTERIES OF SEDONA SERIES:

__Book I — The Mysteries of Sedona . . . . $6.95 $_____

__Book II — The Alien Tide . . . . $7.95 $_____

__Book III — The Quest. . . . . $9.95 $_____

__Book IV — Unseen Beings, Unseen Worlds . . $9.95 $_____

__Book V — Mysterious Sedona . . . . $9.95 $_____

Please include first class postage & handling as follows:
$3 for the first book, $1 each book thereafter. . . . . $_____

TOTAL ENCLOSED $_____

These rates apply to the U.S.A. Only. For orders outside the U.S., please write for rates.

Name _____

Address _____

City _____ State ____ Zip _____

Send your check or money order to:
Mysteries of Sedona, P.O. Box 2571, Sedona, AZ 86339

MYSTERIOUS SEDONA

15 Full Color Pages of the Most Amazing, Unexplainable Photos

COMPILED BY TOM DONGO

1 Paranormal photo taken in 1998 near Sedona, Arizona, by Cheryl Dryfka.

page x

2 Paranormal photo taken near Sedona in 1998 by Anthony Alagna (correction from book). Object is not the moon.

page 10

3 Unknown and unseen creature directly behind girl's head. Photo credit: Linda White Eagle.

page 13

4 New domes at the Phoenix Cement plant, Clarkdale, Arizona.

page 39

5 New domes at the Phoenix Cement plant, Clarkdale, Arizona.

page 39

6 "Ram" paranormal photo taken in 1998 near Sedona by Cheryl Dryfka.

page 50

7 Gift shop vandalized by invisible and unknown creature. Photo taken in 1994 by Linda Bradshaw.

page 63

8 Mysterious light in right center (above treetops) came straight toward the camera. Photo taken in 1997 by Tom Dongo.

page 79

9 Dog killed by a car. The dog reappeared hours later, alive. Photo taken a few weeks later by Tom Dongo.

page 98

10 UFO photo taken near Sedona in 1997 by Karne Snickers.

page 100

11 Bluehaired Man: An unknown and unseen man was not visible when photo was taken. Photo taken in 1995 by Linda Bradshaw.

page 102

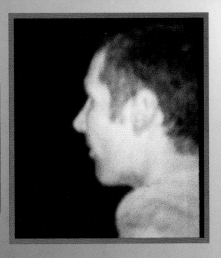

12 Person at left side of photo was not visible at the time the photo was taken. Notice what is in or on "his" right hand. Photo taken in 1994 by Tom Dongo.

page 104

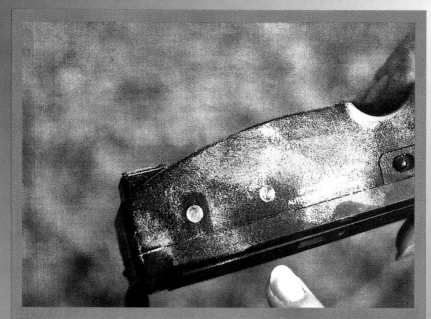

13 Unknown and unseen being's fingerprints on dusted camera. Photo was taken in 1996 by Bob Bradshaw.

page 105

14 Six glowing objects rising from treetops at night. Photo was taken over a 30-minute exposure with a 300 mm lens near Sedona in 1995 by Tom Dongo.

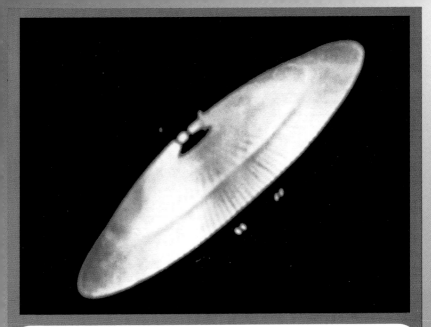

15 Photo taken in Southern California in 1975 by an anonymous photographer.

16 Timed exposure with a 500 mm lens. This was not a campfire. Light was suspended over the trees and blinked off after 5 minutes. Photo taken in 1996 close to Robber's Roost near Sedona by Tom Dongo

17 Photo negative was rigorously examined by photo experts. Determined not to be a hoax or a defect.

18 Unseen to the naked eye. The object is about 75 yards in diameter and is not the moon. Photo taken in Sedona in 1993 by an anonymous photographer.

19

Photos taken near Nashville, Tennessee, on the night of September 27, 1989.

20

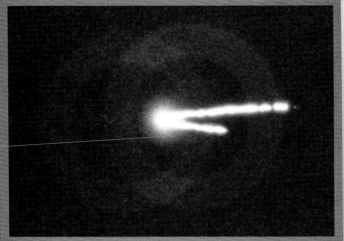

21 Photo lens of 500 mm, 30-second exposure. This only seemed to be one motionless light in the sky when seen by human eyes. The photo revealed more. Photo taken near Sedona in 1996 by Tom Dongo.

This photo was seen by millions of people worldwide on BBC, Japanese and U.S. network television in 1996. These are glowing nighttime objects taking off from the ground in the far distance. Photo taken near Sedona by Tom Dongo with a 5-minute exposure using a 500 mm lens. **22**

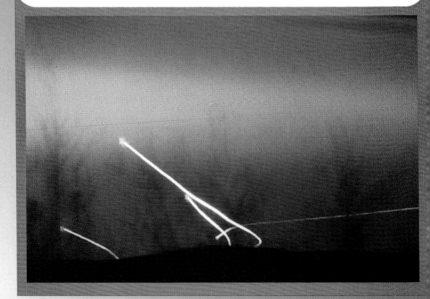

Taken in Boynton Canyon in 1990. This photo was examined by photo experts who concluded that this was not a flaw, fabrication or hoax. Photo by Gloria Reiser.

23

24 This photo was hand delivered to a NASA laboratory in Houston, Texas. It is currently being taken seriously by several NASA scientists, perhaps unofficially. The results may be quite interesting. Photo was taken during the planetary alignment on May 5, 2000, by Renée Propps.